Śākyamuni Buddha

Dharma Master Kumārajīva

Dharma Master Kumārajīva

Nonduality

After each and every Bodhisattva had spoken, they asked Mañjuśrī, "How does the Bodhisattva enter the Dharma-door of nonduality?"

Mañjuśrī said, "As I see it, not to offer words, explanations, comments, or opinions regarding anything and to remain apart from questions and answers is to enter the Dharma-door of nonduality."

Then Mañjuśrī asked Vimalakīrti, "Now that we have all expressed our understanding, what would you, Humane One, say about how a Bodhisattva should enter the Dharma-door of nonduality?"

At that time Vimalakīrti remained silent and did not say a word.

Mañjuśrī exclaimed in praise, "Good indeed, good indeed! To be free even of words and language is truly to enter the Dharma-door of nonduality."

Chapter 9

Entering the Dharma-Door of Nonduality

不二法门

THE DHARMA-DOOR OF NONDUALITY

保開口

TAUGHT IN WORDLESS SILENCE

不二法門

如是諸菩薩各各說已，問文殊師利：「何等是菩薩入不二法門？」

文殊師利曰：「如我意者，於一切法無言無說，無示無識，離諸問答，是為入不二法門。」

於是文殊師利問維摩詰：「我等各自說已，仁者當說，何等是菩薩入不二法門？」

時維摩詰默然無言。

文殊師利歎曰：「善哉！善哉！乃至無有文字、語言，是真入不二法門。」

入不二法門品第九

THE VIMALAKĪRTI SŪTRA

維摩詰所說經

THE VIMALAKĪRTI SŪTRA

維摩詰所說經

TRANSLATED FROM THE CHINESE OF
DHARMA MASTER KUMĀRAJĪVA
(TAISHŌ VOLUME XIV • NO.475)

BY

THE INTERNATIONAL INSTITUTE FOR
THE TRANSLATION OF BUDDHIST TEXTS

BUDDHIST TEXT TRANSLATION SOCIETY
UKIAH, CALIFORNIA

The Vimalakīrti Sūtra
Translated by the International Institute for the Translation of Buddhist Texts
Dharma Realm Buddhist University

Buddhist Text Translation Society
4951 Bodhi Way | Ukiah, CA 95482
www.buddhisttexts.org | info@buddhisttexts.org
ISBN (print): 978-1-64217-107-5 (print)
ISBN (ebook): 978-1-64217-108-2 (ebook)

LIBRARY OF CONGRESS CATALOGING-IN-PUBLICATION DATA

Names: The International Institute for the Translation of Buddhist Texts, translator.
Title: The Vimalakirti Sutra = Weimojie suo shuo jing / The International Institute for the Translation of Buddhist Texts (Dharma Realm Buddhist University).
Other titles: Tripitaka. Sūtrapiṭaka. Vimalakīrtinirdeśa. English. | Weimojie suo shuo jing
Description: First. | Ukiah : Buddhist Text Translation Society, 2021. | Includes index. | Summary: "A new translation of the Vimalakīrti Sūtra. Translated from the Chinese of Kumarajiva (Taisho Vol. XIV. No. 475) by the International Institute for the Translation of Buddhist Texts (IITBT) at Dharma Realm Buddhist University. Also called Vimalakīrti Nirdeśa Sūtra, it dates from no later than the 3rd century CE, and most likely from the 1st or 2nd centuries CE. In the sūtra the layman and householder Vimalakīrti , who is also a model bodhisattva, instructs deities, learned Buddhist arhats, and lay people in all matters concerning the nature of enlightenment, emptiness (sunyata), and non-duality. Vimalakīrti employs a subtle understanding of "skill in means" (upāya) to lead them the highest truth: the counter-intuitive claim that nirvana and saṃsāra, at an ultimate level, are not different. The discourse culminates with a wordless teaching of silence"-- Provided by publisher.
Identifiers: LCCN 2020052477 (print) | LCCN 2020052478 (ebook) | ISBN 9781642171075 (print) | ISBN 9781642171082 (ebook)
Subjects: LCSH: Bodhisattvas. | Bodhisattva (The concept)
Classification: LCC BQ2212.E5 H69 2021 (print) | LCC BQ2212.E5 (ebook) | DDC 294.3/823--dc23
LC record available at https://lccn.loc.gov/2020052477
LC ebook record available at https://lccn.loc.gov/2020052478

CONTENTS

維摩詰所說經目錄

THE EIGHT GUIDELINES OF THE BUDDHIST TEXT TRANSLATION SOCIETY

1. A volunteer must free him/herself from the motives of personal fame and profit.
2. A volunteer must cultivate a respectful and sincere attitude free from arrogance and conceit.
3. A volunteer must refrain from aggrandizing his/her work and denigrating that of others.
4. A volunteer must not establish him/herself as the standard of correctness and suppress the work of others with his or her fault-finding.
5. A volunteer must take the Buddha-mind as his/her own mind.
6. A volunteer must use the wisdom of Dharma-selecting vision to determine true principles.
7. A volunteer must request virtuous elders in the ten directions to certify his/her translations.
8. A volunteer must endeavor to propagate the teachings by printing and distributing *sūtras, śāstra* texts, and *vinaya* texts when the translations are certified as being correct.

FOREWORD

With its many layers of meaning and reference and its cast of fantastic characters, most modern readers will probably want to approach the *Vimalakīrti Sūtra* as a piece of literature: think the magical realism of Márquez's *Hundred Years of Solitude*. The "magic" of such works is not intended as a flight of fancy. Its genius lies in directly expressing something about our actual experience that cannot be captured by a more rational description. What results is not a metaphor, exactly, but its own kind of literary device.

As a literary object, the *Vimalakīrti Sūtra* works very well. Not only does it give an indirect overview of Buddhist schools and teachings, it critiques itself and Buddhist doctrine along the way. It's not quite ironic, but its playfulness and style allow it to examine things in a lighthearted way that counteracts the tendency to dogmatism.

The heart of any Buddhist text is ridding the human consciousness of an inherent dualism. We need to read all the teachings as creating, in one way or another, some Dharma-device that will take people through and beyond their natural propensity for dualism. This propensity is described in detail in the *Śūraṅgama Sūtra;* and for that reason, the *Śūraṅgama* and *Vimalakīrti* read very well together. In fact, the *Vimalakīrti* presents a bit of a danger on its own, if it is not paired with the *Śūraṅgama*. If we don't read it carefully, we could understand it to be saying things it's not really saying—about the role of the lay scholar, for instance.

From early on in Buddhism's entry into China, the *Vimalakīrti* and several other Prajñāpāramitā texts were extremely popular. At that time, the vinaya was not well-established, and knowledgeable translators were very few. The main proponent of Buddhism in China was the wealthy, educated layman, who had free time to hang around, study sūtras, meditate: a rarefied class, to say the least. Vimalakīrti served as a prototype for these people. If you read the sūtra carefully, of course, you see that Vimalakīrti is not a proponent of lay Buddhism. He's just showing up in a certain form to teach people. He's not selling that particular form; he's just using it to teach people not to essentialize.

In this sense, the *Vimalakīrti Sūtra* is an excellent modern work, because it's antiessentialist in every way. It's a kind of postmodern Buddhism; it deessentializes every element of itself and the teachings, and while doing so, it teaches a fundamental Dharma lesson. Within the larger frame of Buddhist texts, the *Vimalakīrti Sūtra* is extremely important because it can correct or give reference to other texts that tend to essentialize the Dharma in ways that the *Vimalakīrti* makes fun of or jokes around with, plays the devil's advocate with. In a bigger picture sense, the Buddhadharma already has this question about language, about presenting anything at all as "Buddhadharma"—this mistake that can be made in setting anything up. To undermine that is crucial to the larger Buddhist message. And the *Vimalakīrti* does that. But by itself, without that context, it's very tricky. If you don't know what it's correcting, you won't understand its critique, and you can get into a lot of trouble and misuse it to make all kinds of points, especially regarding the precepts. It must be read carefully. Otherwise it can be easily misused, especially in the modern context, where antiessentialism has been carried so far, into every sort of situation and institution.

The *Vimalakīrti* is not criticizing the vinaya. It's not criticizing monasticism. If you read it carefully, it's actually a proponent of monasticism; but it can be read from a vantage point that puts lay scholars in a position of authority over everyone else, and seeing through everything. If you read it that way, the text could be seen as lacking an emphasis on the monastic form as a means to discipline the body and mind to be processed through the ten grounds and be effective as a Bodhisattva. Putting the sūtra within its proper frame of reference helps to prevent this kind of misreading.

The Venerable Hsuan Hua's Vision

Buddhism in the modern Western world isn't even at the kindergarten level. But what Master Hua could see at the grand scale was that three things were necessary for Buddhism to come into the West. Not just Buddhism in the West, either. To ensure the future of humanity, there were three essential things: translation, education, and maintaining the monastic tradition. Basically, Master Hua could see that humanity would have to start all over again, from a seed; it might preserve some of what we have now, but it would more or less have to start over.

The first essential element in starting over is to maintain the monastic tradition as a choice. It has to be available as a choice. People only really have two modes of living: at-home and left-home. If you live at home, you have to engage with the conditional at some level; you have to participate in some kind of strategic construct—working for a living or whatever—that will take up some amount of time. As a monastic, that's taken care of. In exchange, you take on the responsibility of maintaining the Dharma in one way or another. As a layperson, you can stay away from spouses and pets as much as you like, but you still have to pay for your apartment and so on; you have to get involved with the conditional, and you can throw in a little meditation here and there. As a monastic, you avoid that—but you have to be a Bodhisattva. That's the trade-off. Master Hua was very clear: when it comes down to it, it's one or the other. Maintaining the monastic tradition is vital, as a practical issue, not a just a metaphysical one. On the one hand, people need to have this choice available to them; on the other, someone needs to maintain the Dharma.

The other two elements—education and translation—are intertwined. Whatever framework of reality is operating within a culture at a given time, it comes primarily through the educational construct. So having a thriving system, from elementary up through post-graduate studies, is indispensable to a healthy future. Translation acts a kind of liaison in that process; it can influence the educational construct and help to create an alternative to the one we have now. We've barely even scratched the surface of translating the Dharma into English. As more texts become available, people will be faced with a lot of different things. The Buddha was very flexible. He taught to all kinds of conditions. As more of the Dharma is brought into English, plenty of opportunities will open up for people to look at things in a new way.

Master Hua wanted to see hundreds of people working together on translation. He wanted to bring people together from all over the world. Like a Borobudur of translation. The problem is our imagination. We think so small. We don't really consider just how big a project this could be, and how many people could work on it together. Master Hua wanted to bring everyone together. If our translation work could be like this, it could really be what he envisioned as an essential part of ensuring a better future for all of us.

Doug Powers
Vice President for Finance and Administration,
Professor, Dharma Realm Buddhist University
September 27, 2020

ACKNOWLEDGMENTS

This project was coordinated by the International Institute for the Translation of Buddhist Texts (IITBT) at Dharma Realm Buddhist University (https://www.drbu.edu/programs/iitbt). The committee wishes to gratefully acknowledge the many people whose talents and dedication lead to the completion of this endeavor. Translation work on this volume began in the summer of 2016, and was resumed in 2018, during IITBT's annual week-long Translation Seminar. The remaining work was undertaken by students and staff of IITBT's Graduate Certificate Program in Buddhist Translation. IITBT staff took primary responsibility for review and editing in the project's final stages.

Contributors are listed below according to the alphabetical order of their first names.

Primary Translation:
Participants of the Translation Seminar (2016, 2018)
Students of the Graduate Certificate Program
(2016, 2019–2020)
Michael Lu

Review Committee:
Students of the Graduate Certificate Program
(2019–2020)
Qin Feng Ling
Yang Liu

Editorial Committee:
Justin Howe

Cover Design:
Bhikṣuṇī Heng Yi

Interior Design:
Ākāśa
Dennis Crean

Illustration:
Cathie Chen
Qianhe Man

Layout:
Ākāśa
Dennis Crean

Graphic Design:
Bhikṣuṇī Heng Yi

Graphic Production:
Ākāśa
Cathie Chen
Jerry Chen
Bhikṣuṇī Jin An
Wendy Chen

Certification:
Bhikṣuṇī Heng Yi

EDITORIAL & TECHNICAL NOTES

This new English-language translation of the *Vimalakīrti Sūtra* is based on Master Kumārajīva's Chinese translation. Although a Sanskrit version of the sūtra (thought lost for centuries) was recently discovered, it is not certain that Master Kumārajīva's translation was based on that text.

This bilingual volume contains the sūtra text in both English and Chinese. Throughout the margin of the text, reference numbers appear to assist the reader in cross-referencing the English and Chinese versions. Numbers given for the English text refer to the same passage of sūtra text in Chinese and vice versa. For instance, 7.075 would refer to chapter 7, passage 75. These reference numbers have been assigned by the editors for the reader's convenience, and are not part of the original sūtra.

Throughout the text, prose passages with a regular, repeating formula have been set apart with hanging indents. This choice was made by the editors to enhance readability and does not reflect a feature of the Chinese text.

Pinyin is used for the romanization of Chinese words. Sanskrit words and names have been romanized with diacritical marks unless they are treated as English words: for example, Bodhisattva, Buddha, Dharma, karma, and so on.

Verse for Opening a Sūtra

The unsurpassed, profound, and
wonderful Dharma,
Is difficult to encounter in hundreds
of millions of eons,
I now see and hear it, receive and uphold it,
And I vow to fathom the Tathāgata's
true meaning

THE VIMALAKĪRTI SŪTRA

維摩詰所說經

BUDDHALANDS

CHAPTER 1

Thus I have heard. At one time the Buddha dwelt in the garden of Āmrapālī near Vaiśālī, together with a great assembly of eight thousand bhikṣus. There were also thirty-two thousand Bodhisattvas who were recognized by the assembly and who had perfected their great wisdom and foundational practices by virtue of all Buddhas' awe-inspiring spiritual powers. As strongholds of the Dharma, they upheld the Proper Dharma; roaring the lion's roar, they were renowned throughout the ten directions.

These Bodhisattvas befriended others and offered 1.001
comfort without being asked. Enabling the Three Jewels to flourish and continue, they subdued demons and brought cults and deviant practitioners under control. Completely purified, they had transcended all hindrances and fetters. They constantly settled their minds in unobstructed liberation. Their mindfulness, samādhi, total retention, and eloquence were everlasting. They had perfected giving, upholding precepts, patience, vigor, dhyāna, wisdom, and the power of

skillful means. Having realized nonattainment, the patient acceptance of the nonarising of phenomena, they were able to turn the irreversible wheel in accord with circumstances.

Skillfully comprehending the characteristics of all phenomena, they understood the faculties of living beings. They sheltered the great assembly, who thereby became fearless. They cultivated their minds by means of merit and wisdom. Graced with exquisite hallmarks, their bodies were supreme; they had renounced all worldly adornments. They were known far and wide, above and beyond even Mount Sumeru. Their profound faith was resolute like vajra. Their Dharma treasures illuminated everywhere as they rained down sweet dew. Among the languages and voices of living beings, theirs were most subtle and wonderful. Profoundly comprehending dependent arising, they had cut off all wrong views, emptied the two extremes of existence and nonexistence, and put an end to all residual habit energies. Like lions roaring, they proclaimed the Dharma without fear; and their exposition resounded like thunder, without limits and beyond all limits.

1.002 Like captains at sea, they had amassed troves of Dharma treasures. They thoroughly understood the profound and wondrous principles of all phenomena. They fully understood the past and future lives and thoughts of living beings. They were not far from the Buddhas' unparalleled wisdom of self-mastery, ten powers,[1] [four kinds of] fearlessness,[2] and eighteen unique attributes.[3] Though having closed all doors to the lower destinies, they nevertheless took rebirth in the five paths. They were like great physician kings who skillfully prescribe medicine appropriate to a myriad of ailments, urging it to be taken. Having perfected limitless merit, they had adorned and purified countless Buddhalands. All those who saw and heard them gained benefit. Nothing they did was done in vain. They were replete with all merits such as these.

Their names were Bodhisattva Contemplating All as Equal, Bodhisattva Contemplating All as Distinct, Bodhisattva Contemplating All as Equal and Distinct, Bodhisattva King of Self-Mastery in Samādhi, Bodhisattva King of Self-Mastery in the Dharma, Bodhisattva Characteristic of Dharma, Bodhisattva Luminous Characteristic, Bodhisattva Radiant Splendor, Bodhisattva Magnificent Splendor, Bodhisattva Accumulation of Treasures, Bodhisattva Accumulation of Eloquence, Bodhisattva Jeweled Hands, Bodhisattva Jeweled Mudrā, Bodhisattva Constantly Raised Hands, Bodhisattva Constantly Lowered Hands, Bodhisattva Who Shows Constant Sympathy, Bodhisattva Roots of Bliss, Bodhisattva King of Bliss, Bodhisattva Eloquent Voice, Bodhisattva Treasury of Emptiness, Bodhisattva Jeweled Torch Bearer, Bodhisattva Jeweled Valor, Bodhisattva Jeweled Insight, Bodhisattva Indra's Net, Bodhisattva Net of Illumination, Bodhisattva Contemplation Free from Conditions, Bodhisattva Accumulation of Wisdom, Bodhisattva Supreme Treasure, Bodhisattva Heavenly King, Bodhisattva Annihilator of Demons, Bodhisattva Lightning-Like Virtue, Bodhisattva King of Self-Mastery, Bodhisattva Adorned with Merit, Bodhisattva Lion's Roar, Bodhisattva Thunderous Voice, Bodhisattva Din of Colliding Mountains, Bodhisattva Fragrant Elephant, Bodhisattva Fragrant White Elephant, Bodhisattva Constant Vigor, Bodhisattva Never Resting, Bodhisattva Born of Wonder, Bodhisattva Flower Garland, Bodhisattva Who Contemplates the World's Sounds, Bodhisattva Great Strength, Bodhisattva Brahmā's Net, Bodhisattva Jeweled Scepter, Bodhisattva Invincible, Bodhisattva Adorned Lands, Bodhisattva Golden Topknot, Bodhisattva Pearl Topknot, Bodhisattva Maitreya, Bodhisattva Dharma Prince Mañjuśrī, and other Bodhisattvas such as these, thirty-two thousand in all. 1.003

1.004 In addition, ten thousand kings of the Brahmā Heavens, Śikhin and others, came from other world systems to listen to the Buddha teach the Dharma. Furthermore, twelve thousand Śakras from other world systems came to join the assembly. Immensely powerful gods, dragons, spirits, yakṣas, gandharvas, asuras, garuḍas, kiṃnaras, and mahoragas all came to join the assembly, together with bhikṣus, bhikṣuṇīs, upāsakas, and upāsikās, who also came to join the assembly.

At that time the Buddha taught the Dharma to the countless hundreds of thousands of beings who were reverently surrounding him. He was like Sumeru, the king of mountains, looming high above the ocean, as he sat peacefully upon his many-jeweled lion throne, outshining all those who had assembled.

At that time the son of an elder of Vaiśālī, whose name was Accumulation of Treasures, along with the sons of five hundred elders, each carrying a canopy of the seven treasures, came to pay their respects to the Buddha. Bowing their heads at the Buddha's feet, they offered him their canopies. By means of the Buddha's awe-inspiring spiritual powers, all these priceless canopies joined together into a single canopy covering the entire trichiliocosm, whose whole length and breadth were manifest within it. Within this priceless canopy appeared all of the trichiliocosm's Mount Sumerus, Snow Mountains, Mucilinda Mountains, Mahāmucilinda Mountains, Incense Mountains, Jeweled Mountains, Gold Mountains, Black Mountains, Ring of Iron Mountains, and Great Ring of Iron Mountains; all of its seas, rivers, streams, and springs, as well as its suns, moons, and celestial bodies; and all its palaces of gods, dragons, and spirits.

In addition, all Buddhas teaching the Dharma throughout the ten directions appeared within this priceless canopy. Seeing the Buddha's spiritual powers, the great assembly praised them as unprecedented. They placed their palms together and bowed to the Buddha, gazing up at him reverently without averting their eyes for even a moment.

1.005 Then the elder's son Accumulation of Treasures spoke in verse:

The Buddha's eyes are as pure and broad as
blue lotuses.
His pure mind transcends even all samādhis.
Long has he accumulated limitless pure karma.
Because he guides beings by means of stillness,
we bow to him.

We see the great sage, through spiritual transformations, make appear
Within this canopy countless Buddhalands of the
ten directions;
And in these lands, we see the Buddhas teach the
Dharma.
All of this we see and hear.

The Dharma King with Dharma power rescues
living beings,
Constantly giving Dharma wealth to each and
every one.
Skillfully discerning the characteristics of all
phenomena,
He dwells unwavering in the supreme truth
And has attained self-mastery of all phenomena.
Thus we bow our heads before the Dharma King.

He teaches neither the existence nor the nonexistence of phenomena,
Which come into being only through dependent
origination.

There is no self, agent, or recipient of action, yet good and bad karma,
Once created, continue on until they are fulfilled.

1.006 When the Buddha conquered Marā beneath the bodhi tree,
He realized the sweet dew of stillness and awakened to the Way.
Having relinquished sense perception, cognition,
And mental formations, he vanquishes all outside ways.

Three times the Buddha turned the inherently
And eternally pure Dharma wheel in this trichiliocosm;
The gods who realized the Way thereupon bore witness
To the appearance of the Three Jewels in the world.

With his wondrous Dharma, the Buddha rescues living beings.
Having awakened, he will never retreat, and ever abides in stillness.
The great physician king saves beings from old age, sickness, and death.
All should pay respects to the ocean of Dharma, boundless in its virtue.

Unmoving as Mount Sumeru in the face of praise and blame,
He is equally compassionate to good and bad alike;
His mind is impartial like empty space. Who could hear
The jewel among people and fail to pay respects?

We now offer to the World Honored One 1.007
This humble canopy in which the trichiliocosm
Is shown to us, with all its palaces of gods,
Dragons, spirits, yakṣas, and gandharvas.

Everything in the world is made visible
By the grace of the Ten Powers' transformations;[4]
All those who see this praise the Buddha.
Now we bow our heads before the one honored in all three realms.

The great sage, the Dharma King, is a refuge for the multitude.
Beholding the Buddha with a pure mind, everyone is overjoyed.
Each sees the World Honored One appear before them.
Such are the spiritual powers unique to the Buddha.

The Buddha expounds the Dharma in a single voice;
Living beings understand it according to their capacities.
Each believes the World Honored One is speaking to them.
Such are the spiritual powers unique to the Buddha.

The Buddha expounds the Dharma in a single voice;
Each living being understands it in their own way.
Practicing and upholding it, each gains their own benefit.
Such are the spiritual powers unique to the Buddha.

1.008 The Buddha expounds the Dharma in a single voice;
Some feel fear, some feel joy,
Some grow disillusioned, and some sever doubt.
Such are the spiritual powers unique to the Buddha.

Bow before the Ten Powers, the greatly vigorous one.
Bow before the one who has realized fearlessness.
Bow before the one anchored in the unique attributes.
Bow before the great guiding master of all.
Bow before the one who has severed all bonds and fetters.
Bow before the one who has arrived at the other shore.
Bow before the one who rescues beings in all worlds.
Bow before the one who has forever transcended samsaric paths.

Completely knowing the past and future lives of every living being,
The Buddha skillfully liberates himself from all phenomena.
Detaching himself from the mundane world like a lotus,
He ever skillfully engages in the practice of emptiness and stillness.
He comprehends without impediment the characteristics of all phenomena.
Bow before the one who relies on nothing, like empty space.

Then, after the elder's son Accumulation of Treasures had spoken these verses, he said to the Buddha, "World Honored One! Each of these five hundred elders' sons has resolved upon anuttarā samyaksaṃbodhi. We wish to hear about the purity of Buddhalands. We sincerely hope that the World Honored One will explain to us the Bodhisattvas' practice of purifying Buddhalands." 1.009

The Buddha said, "Good indeed, Accumulation of Treasures! For the sake of all the Bodhisattvas, you ask about the practices that purify the Tathāgatas' lands. Listen closely, listen closely! Consider this well; I will now explain it for you!"

Accumulation of Treasures and the five hundred elders' sons then listened as instructed.

The Buddha said, "Accumulation of Treasures! Bodhisattvas shape their Buddhalands in response to the various kinds of living beings. In what way? According to the living beings they teach, Bodhisattvas shape their Buddhalands. According to the living beings they tame and subdue, Bodhisattvas shape their Buddhalands. According to what kinds of lands will lead living beings to enter into the Buddhas' wisdom, Bodhisattvas shape their Buddhalands. According to what kinds of lands will lead living beings to develop a Bodhisattva's roots, Bodhisattvas shape their Buddhalands.

"Why is this? Bodhisattvas create pure lands for the sole purpose of benefiting all living beings. For example, someone wishing to build a palace on empty land could do as they pleased. But to build a palace in empty space would be impossible. In the same way, Bodhisattvas vow to create Buddhalands for the sake of leading living beings to ultimate realization. The vow to create Buddhalands cannot be based on empty space.

1.010 Accumulation of Treasures, understand that a forthright mind is the Bodhisattva's pure land. After Bodhisattvas realize Buddhahood, honest living beings are born in those Bodhisattvas' lands.

A mind profoundly engrossed in the truth is the Bodhisattva's pure land. After Bodhisattvas realize Buddhahood, living beings who have perfected their merit are born in those Bodhisattvas' lands.

The bodhi resolve is the Bodhisattva's pure land. After Bodhisattvas realize Buddhahood, living beings of the Great Vehicle are born in those Bodhisattvas' lands.

Giving is the Bodhisattva's pure land. After Bodhisattvas realize Buddhahood, living beings disposed to giving are born in those Bodhisattvas' lands.

Upholding precepts is the Bodhisattva's pure land. After Bodhisattvas realize Buddhahood, living beings who have fulfilled their vows by perfecting the ten wholesome deeds are born in those Bodhisattvas' lands.

Patience is the Bodhisattva's pure land. After Bodhisattvas realize Buddhahood, living beings adorned with the thirty-two hallmarks are born in those Bodhisattvas' lands.

Vigor is the Bodhisattva's pure land. After Bodhisattvas realize Buddhahood, living beings who diligently cultivate all merit and virtue are born in those Bodhisattvas' lands.

Dhyāna is the Bodhisattva's pure land. After Bodhisattvas realize Buddhahood, living beings with minds concentrated and unperturbed are born in those Bodhisattvas' lands.

Wisdom is the Bodhisattva's pure land. After Bodhisattvas realize Buddhahood, living beings with right concentration are born in those Bodhisattvas' lands. 1.011

The four infinite states of mind are the Bodhisattva's pure land. After Bodhisattvas realize Buddhahood, living beings who have perfected kindness, compassion, joy, and equanimity are born in those Bodhisattvas' lands.

The four methods of attraction are the Bodhisattva's pure land. After Bodhisattvas realize Buddhahood, living beings who have been liberated through these four means are born in those Bodhisattvas' lands.

Skillful means are the Bodhisattva's pure land. After Bodhisattvas realize Buddhahood, living beings whose use of skillful means is unobstructed in all circumstances are born in those Bodhisattvas' lands.

The thirty-seven factors of awakening are the Bodhisattva's pure land. After Bodhisattvas realize Buddhahood, living beings who have perfected the [four] foundations of mindfulness, the [four] kinds of right effort, the [four] steps to spiritual powers, the [five] roots, the [five] powers, the [seven] factors of awakening, and the [eightfold] path[5] are born in those Bodhisattvas' lands.

A heart of dedication is the Bodhisattva's pure land. After Bodhisattvas realize Buddhahood, they realize a land perfect in merit.

1.012 The instruction for eradicating the eight difficulties[6] is the Bodhisattva's pure land. After Bodhisattvas realize Buddhahood, their lands are without the three lower destinies and the eight difficulties.

Upholding precepts without criticizing the faults of others is the Bodhisattva's pure land. After Bodhisattvas realize Buddhahood, their lands are without even the words 'infraction' and 'prohibition.'

The ten wholesome deeds are the Bodhisattva's pure land. After Bodhisattvas realize Buddhahood, living beings who do not die prematurely, who possess great wealth, who maintain pure conduct, who speak truthfully, who speak gently, who inspire loyalty in their followers, who can skillfully mediate disputes, who speak only beneficial words, who are never jealous or angry, or who hold right views[7] are born in those Bodhisattvas' lands.

Thus, Accumulation of Treasures, as Bodhisattvas' minds are made forthright, their practice is established.

As their practice is established, they realize minds profoundly engrossed in the truth.

As their minds become profoundly engrossed in the truth, they discipline their minds.

As they discipline their minds, they practice according to the teachings.

As they practice according to the teachings, they make dedications.

As they make dedications, they establish their skillful means.

As they establish their skillful means, they lead
living beings to ultimate realization.
As they lead living beings to ultimate realization,
they purify their Buddhalands.
As they purify their Buddhalands, they purify
their exposition of the Dharma.
As they purify their exposition of the Dharma,
they purify their wisdom.
As they purify their wisdom, they purify their
minds.
And as they purify their minds, they purify all
merit and virtue.

"Therefore, Accumulation of Treasures, if Bodhisattvas wish to attain pure lands, they must first purify their minds. As they purify their minds, they purify their Buddhalands."

At that time, aided by the Buddha's awe-inspiring 1.013
spiritual powers, Śāriputra thought, "Supposing that as Bodhisattvas purify their minds, they purify their Buddhalands, then when our World Honored One was a Bodhisattva, was his mind not pure? How else could this land come to be so impure?"

Knowing his thoughts, the Buddha said to Śāriputra, "What do you think? Is it because the sun and moon are impure that the blind cannot see them?"

Śāriputra replied, "By no means, World Honored One! It is the problem of the blind, not the problem of the sun and moon."

"Śāriputra, it is because of their offenses that living beings are blind to the splendid purity of the Tathāgata's Buddhaland. The Tathāgata is not to blame! Śāriputra, my land is pure, but you do not see it."

1.014 Then Brahmā Spiral Topknot said to Śāriputra, "Do not think that this Buddhaland is impure! Why not? I perceive Śakyamuni's Buddhaland to be as pure as the heavenly palace of Sovereign Ease."

Śāriputra replied, "I see in this land hills and hollows, thorns and gravel, rocks and mountains—defilement and evil are everywhere!"

Brahmā Spiral Topknot said, "Humane One, your mind is subject to high and low and does not follow the Buddhas' wisdom; therefore, you perceive this land as impure. Śāriputra! Bodhisattvas who regard all living beings equally, whose minds are pure and deeply engrossed in the truth, and who follow the Buddhas' wisdom perceive this Buddhaland as pure."

The Buddha then touched his toe to the earth, and immediately the trichiliocosm was magnificently adorned with hundreds of thousands of precious treasures, just like the land of Buddha Jeweled Adornment, the Land Adorned with Treasures of Limitless Merit and Virtue. The entire great assembly was amazed by this unprecedented event, and all saw themselves seated upon jeweled lotus flowers.

The Buddha then said to Śāriputra, "Do you now perceive the splendid purity of this Buddhaland?"

Śāriputra replied, "Yes I do, World Honored One! I was unable to see or hear it before, but now the splendid purity of this Buddhaland is apparent."

The Buddha said to Śāriputra, "My Buddhaland is always pure like this. I only make it appear rife with evil and impurity for the sake of saving living beings of lowly aspirations. This is akin to how the gods all eat from the same jeweled vessel, but their food appears differently depending on their merit and virtue. In the same way, Śāriputra, a person whose mind is pure will see this land as adorned with merit."

After the Buddha manifested the splendid purity of his land, Accumulation of Treasures and the five hundred elders' sons all realized the patient acceptance of the non-arising of phenomena, while eighty-four thousand people all resolved upon anuttarā samyaksaṃbodhi. The Buddha then withdrew his toe, and the world reverted to the way it was before. Thirty-two thousand gods and humans who sought the Śrāvaka Vehicle understood the impermanence of all conditioned phenomena, forever transcended all defilement, and attained the clarity of the Dharma eye with respect to all phenomena. And the eight thousand bhikṣus detached themselves from all phenomena, ended their outflows, and attained freedom of mind.

SKILLFUL MEANS

CHAPTER 2

At that time an elder by the name of Vimalakīrti was living in the great city of Vaiśāli. In the past he had made offerings to countless Buddhas, established deep good roots, attained the patient acceptance of the nonarising of phenomena, attained unobstructed eloquence, realized the mastery of spiritual play, mastered total retention, attained fearlessness, and conquered demonic troubles and resentment. He had delved deeply into every Dharma-door, mastered the perfection of wisdom, become proficient in skillful means, and fulfilled all great vows. Knowing the inclinations of living beings' minds, he could discern their keen and dull faculties. Having mastered the practices leading to Buddhahood, he was firmly established in the Great Vehicle. He was deliberate in his every action. Perfectly maintaining the Buddhas' awe-inspiring deportment, his mind was as vast as the sea. All Buddhas praised him profusely, and he was revered by all Śrāvakas, Śakras, brahmās, and four heavenly kings.

Wishing to rescue living beings through the use of skillful means, he dwelt in Vaiśāli. With boundless wealth, he gathered in the poor; in his perfect observation of the precepts, he gathered in the misguided; tempering his conduct with patience, he gathered in the hateful; with great vigor, he gathered in the lazy; in his single-minded meditative concentration, he gathered in the unfocused; and with ultimate wisdom, he gathered in the foolish.

2.015 Although he wore a white robe,[8] he reverently upheld a śramaṇa's pure precepts and practices.
Although he was a householder, he remained unattached to the three realms.
Although appearing to have a wife and children, he constantly practiced pure conduct.
Although appearing to be a householder, he took delight in solitude.
Although he decked himself in lavish jewels and finery, the hallmarks were his true adornments.
Although he ate and drank, his true nourishment was dhyāna bliss.

When he went to places where people played games of skill and chance, he went there only to liberate them.
Although he studied non-Buddhist teachings, his faith was proper and did not falter.
Although he understood works of secular writing, the Buddhadharma was his constant joy.
Respected by all, he was most worthy of offerings.
Upholding the Proper Dharma, he gathered in both young and old.

Although his enterprises were successful, he took no delight in worldly profit and gain. 2.016
Frequenting busy thoroughfares, he benefited living beings.
He participated in government to protect and safeguard the people.
Going to places of lecture and debate, he led living beings to the Great Vehicle.
Visiting schools, he edified and inspired the students.
Going to brothels, he made people aware of the follies of desire.
Visiting taverns and public houses, he helped the patrons establish clarity of purpose.

Most revered when he appeared among the elders, he taught them the supreme Dharma.
Most revered when he appeared among the laypeople, he cut off their attachments.
Most revered when he appeared among the kṣatriyas, he taught them patience.
Most revered when he appeared among the brāhmaṇas, he rid them of their arrogance. 2.017
Most revered when he appeared among the ministers, he taught them upright conduct.
Most revered when he appeared among the princes, he taught them loyalty and filial respect.
Most revered when he appeared among the mentors of the palace women, he transformed the ladies-in-waiting.
Most revered when he appeared among the commoners, he inspired them to cultivate merit.

Most revered when he appeared among the
Brahmā gods, he guided them toward
supreme wisdom.
Most revered when he appeared among Śakras,
he manifested impermanence.
Most revered when he appeared among the four
heavenly kings, he safeguarded living beings.

In this way the elder Vimalakīrti employed countless skillful means to benefit living beings. As an expedient, he manifested illness to teach the kings, ministers, elders, laypeople, brāhmaṇas, princes, officers, and so on—all of the many thousands who came to inquire about his health. To all those who came to visit him, Vimalakīrti used the occasion of his illness to extensively explain the Dharma, saying, "Humane Ones! The body is impermanent, feeble, weak, and fragile. It quickly rots away and cannot be relied upon! It is host to suffering, worry, and all kinds of diseases.

2.018 "Humane Ones! The wise do not rely upon a body like this.

The body is like foam, which cannot be grasped
and held.
The body is like a bubble; it does not last.
The body is like a mirage, born of thirst and
longing.
The body is like a plantain tree, with nothing
solid inside.
The body is like an illusion, arising from
confusion.
The body is like a dream, empty and unreal.
The body is like a shadow, manifesting from karmic conditions.
The body is like an echo, a confluence of causes
and conditions.

The body is like a drifting cloud, changing and vanishing in an instant.
The body is like lightning, not abiding for even a moment.

Like earth, the body has no master.
Like fire, the body has no self.
Like wind, the body has no life span.
Like water, the body has no person.[9]

The body is unreal, born of the four elements. 2.019
The body is empty, apart from a self and what pertains to a self.
The body is insensate, like grass, trees, gravel, and debris.
The body cannot act on its own, being driven by the wind.[10]
The body is impure, rife with filth.
The body is illusory: though you wash, clothe, and feed it, it will eventually waste away.
The body is a curse, vexed by one hundred one illnesses.
The body is like a dry well, hemmed in by old age.
The body is unstable, doomed to die.
The body is like venomous snakes, ruthless bandits, and an empty village; it is an assemblage of [the five] skandhas, [the eighteen] sense realms, and [the six] sense gates.[11]

"Humane Ones! This body is disgusting indeed. You should wish for the body of a Buddha. Why? The Buddha's body is the Dharma body. It is born from limitless merit and wisdom; from precepts, samādhi, and wisdom; from liberation and the vision attained in liberation; from kindness, compassion, joy, and equanimity; from the pāramitās of giving, upholding precepts, patience, gentleness, diligent vigor, meditative concentration, liberation, samādhi, erudition, and wisdom; from skillful means, the six spiritual powers, the three spiritual insights,[12] the thirty-seven factors of awakening, calming and contemplation, the ten powers, the four kinds of fearlessness, and the eighteen unique attributes; from relinquishing everything unwholesome and gathering in everything wholesome; from ultimate reality; and from nonindulgence. The Tathāgata's body is born from countless pure practices such as these. Humane Ones! If you wish to attain the Buddha's body and to eliminate the illness afflicting living beings, then you must resolve upon anuttarā samyaksaṃbodhi!"

In this way, the elder Vimalakīrti, teaching Dharma that was suitable to those who came to inquire about his health, inspired many thousands of people to resolve upon anuttarā samyaksaṃbodhi.

ŚRĀVAKAS

CHAPTER 3

At that time the elder Vimalakīrti thought, "I am sick and bedridden. Why hasn't the World Honored One, in his great compassion, shown me sympathy?"

The Buddha, knowing Vimalakīrti's thoughts, straightaway told Śāriputra, "Go visit with Vimalakīrti and inquire about his health."

Śāriputra told the Buddha, "World Honored One! 3.020
I am not fit to go and inquire about his health. Why not? Once, when I was in the forest, sitting in meditation under a tree, Vimalakīrti approached me and said, 'Śāriputra, you do not have to sit to meditate. What is meditation? Meditation is not to manifest body or mind in any of the three realms. Meditation is to remain in the samādhi of cessation of sense perception and cognition while engaging in the activities of everyday life. Meditation is to live the life of an ordinary person without abandoning the practice of the Path. Meditation is when the mind neither settles within nor without. Meditation is to remain unmoved by views while cultivating

the thirty-seven factors of awakening. Meditation is to enter nirvāṇa without severing the afflictions. Whoever can meditate like this will receive the Buddhas' seal of approval.'

"Hearing his words, World Honored One, I was speechless, unable to respond. Therefore, I am not fit to go and inquire about Vimalakīrti's health."

3.021 Then the Buddha told Mahāmaudgalyāyana, "Go visit with Vimalakīrti and inquire about his health."

Mahāmaudgalyāyana told the Buddha, "World Honored One! I am not fit to go and inquire about his health. Why not? Once, in the streets of the great city of Vaiśālī, when I was teaching the Dharma to a group of laypeople, Vimalakīrti approached me and said, 'Mahāmaudgalyāyana, when you teach the Dharma to white-robed laypeople, you should not teach them in the way that you have been. When teaching the Dharma, you should teach according to the Dharma.

Because it departs from the defilement of living
beings, the Dharma is without living beings.
Because it departs from the defilement of self,
the Dharma is without self.
Because it transcends birth and death,
the Dharma is without life span.
Because past and future are cut off,
the Dharma is without people.
Because it is devoid of characteristics,
the Dharma is eternally still.
Because it is independent of conditions,
the Dharma is free of characteristics.
Because language is cut off,
the Dharma is devoid of names.
Because it is apart from cognitive discrimination,
the Dharma cannot be expressed.

Because it is like empty space,
the Dharma is formless.
Because it is ultimately empty,
the Dharma is beyond debate.
Because it is apart from self and what pertains to a self, the Dharma is free from self and what pertains to a self.
Because it transcends consciousness,
the Dharma is without discrimination.
Because it is not relative,
the Dharma is devoid of comparison.
Because it is independent of conditions,
the Dharma is not subject to causation.
Because it is one with all phenomena,
the Dharma accords with true thusness.[13]
Because there is nothing it accords with,
the Dharma is in accord with true thusness.
Because it remains unmoved by extremes, 3.022
the Dharma abides in ultimate reality.
Because it is independent of the six kinds of dust,[14] the Dharma is unmoving.
Because it abides nowhere,
the Dharma neither comes nor goes.

The Dharma accords with emptiness; it accords with the absence of characteristics; it accords with nonaction.
The Dharma goes beyond the attractive and the repulsive.
The Dharma neither grows nor diminishes, is neither created nor destroyed, and relies on nothing.
The Dharma transcends eyes, ears, nose, tongue, body, and mind.

The Dharma has neither above nor below,
remains forever in stillness, and transcends
all contemplative practices.

"'Mahāmaudgalyāyana! Since the Dharma is like this, how can it be explained? When people teach the Dharma, nothing is taught or explained; when people hear the Dharma, nothing is heard or attained. It is like an illusory person teaching the Dharma to illusory people. You should teach the Dharma with this understanding. Understand that the faculties of living beings can be sharp or dull. Be without obstruction in the skillful realization of knowledge and vision. With a heart of great compassion, praise the Great Vehicle. Repay the Buddhas' kindness and never allow the Three Jewels to come to an end. Then teach the Dharma.'

"When Vimalakīrti said this, eight hundred laypeople brought forth the resolve for anuttarā samyaksaṃbodhi. But I myself lack such eloquence. Therefore, I am not fit to go and inquire about Vimalakīrti's health."

3.023 Then the Buddha told Mahākāśyapa, "Go visit with Vimalakīrti and inquire about his health."

Mahākāśyapa told the Buddha, "World Honored One! I am not fit to go and inquire about Vimalakīrti's health. Why not? Once, when I was on alms round in a poor village, Vimalakīrti approached me and said, 'Mahākāśyapa, your heart, though kind and compassionate, is not yet all-encompassing. You abandon the wealthy and request alms only from the poor. Kāśyapa! You should be impartial and follow the proper order during your alms round. One goes on alms round in order to detach from food. One portions out food into morsels in order to break apart the aggregates.[15] One receives food in order to detach from the notion of receiving. Enter a village as though it were fundamentally empty. Regard form as though you were blind. Hear sound as though it were echoes. Consider smell as though it were the wind. Taste flavor without discrimination. Experience tangible sensation as the realization of wisdom. Understand that phenomena are like illusions, lacking both an intrinsic essence and an essence dependent on others. That which does not arise does not cease to be.[16]

"'Kāśyapa! If you can attain the eight kinds of liberation[17] without renouncing the eight improper practices;[18] if you can enter the Proper Dharma through the improper; and if, with a single share of alms, you can give to all living beings and make offerings to all Buddhas, sages, and worthy ones, then you may eat. Those who perform their alms round in this way are neither entangled in nor transcend afflictions, neither enter into nor emerge from samādhi, and neither abide in the world nor remain in nirvāṇa. Those who give do not generate either great or small merit, gaining nothing, losing nothing. This is the proper way to Buddhahood, which does not rely on Śrāvaka practices. Kāśyapa! If you can eat like this, the food will not be given in vain.'

"Hearing his words, World Honored One, I experienced what I never had before. I felt profound reverence for all Bodhisattvas. Then I thought, 'Although this person is a householder, he has such great eloquence and wisdom! Hearing him speak, who would not resolve upon anuttarā samyaksaṃbodhi?' Since then, I have never again encouraged others to undertake Śrāvaka or Pratyekabuddha practices. Therefore, I am not fit to go and inquire about Vimalakīrti's health."

Then the Buddha told Subhūti, "Go visit with 3.024
Vimalakīrti and inquire about his health."

Subhūti told the Buddha, "World Honored One! I am not fit to go and inquire about Vimalakīrti's health. Why not? Once, when I visited his house on alms round, Vimalakīrti took my bowl, filled it with food, and said to me, 'Subhūti! If you can regard all food equally, all phenomena will also be equal. If all phenomena are equal, you will be able to regard all food equally. If you can practice alms round like this, then you can accept food.

"'Subhūti! If you neither cut off sexual desire, anger, and ignorance nor associate with them; if, without doing away with the body, you accord with thusness; if, without putting an end to ignorance and craving, you bring forth insight and liberation; if you attain liberation through the five heinous crimes yet are neither liberated nor bound; if you neither see the four noble truths nor fail to see them; if you neither attain fruition nor fail to attain fruition; if you are neither of the world nor apart from the world; if you are neither a sage nor not a sage; if, while perfecting every practice, you remain apart from them—if you can be like this, then you can accept food.

3.025 "'Subhūti! If, neither having seen the Buddha nor heard the Dharma, you leave home under the six non-Buddhist teachers—Pūraṇa Kāśyapa, Maskarin Gośālīputra, Saṃjayin Vairaṭīputra, Ajita Keśakambala, Kakuda Kātyāyana, and Nirgrantha Jñātiputra[19]—and follow them even when they fall, then you can accept food.

"'Subhūti! If you adopt improper views and do not arrive at the other shore; if you remain among the eight difficulties and do not attain freedom from them; if you unite with afflictions and leave behind pure practices; if, when you attain the samādhi of noncontention, all living beings attain the same samādhi; if those who give to you are not sowing a field of blessings; if those who make offerings to you fall into the three lower destinies; if you join hands with the hordes of demons and keep company with the afflictions, and if you are no different from them; if you resent all living beings, slander the Buddha, defame the Dharma, abandon the Sangha, and never realize nirvāṇa—if you can be like this, then you can accept food.'

"Hearing his words, World Honored One, I was at a loss. I could not understand what he had said and did not know how to respond, so I put down my bowl and tried to leave his house. But Vimalakīrti said, 'Subhūti, have no fear! Take your bowl. What do you think? If a person conjured by the Tathāgata confronted you with matters such as these, would you be afraid?'

"'No,' I replied.

"Vimalakīrti said, 'Every phenomenon is like an illusion. So do not be afraid. Why not? Words and language are also like this. The wise do not attach to words; therefore, they are fearless. Why? Words have no intrinsic nature of their own; their nonexistence is just liberation, by which all phenomena are characterized.'

"When Vimalakīrti said this, two hundred gods attained the clarity of the Dharma eye with respect to all phenomena. Therefore, I am not fit to go and inquire about Vimalakīrti's health."

Then the Buddha told Pūrṇamaitrāyaṇīputra, "Go 3.026
visit with Vimalakīrti and inquire about his health."

Pūrṇa told the Buddha, "World Honored One! I am not fit to go and inquire about Vimalakīrti's health. Why not? Once, when I was sitting under a tree in the forest, teaching the Dharma to a group of newly ordained bhikṣus, Vimalakīrti approached me and said, 'Pūrṇa! Before teaching them the Dharma, you should enter samādhi and observe their minds. Do not put putrid food in a precious vessel. You must understand the minds of these bhikṣus; do not treat vaiḍūrya as though it were glass. You do not understand the fundamental potential of living beings; do not inspire them with the Lesser Vehicle Dharma. Do not cut into the flesh of those who are free of sores and lesions. Do not point out a small byway to those who wish to walk the great path. Do not attempt to pour the great ocean into the hoofprint of an ox. Do not equate the light of the sun with the glow of a firefly. Pūrṇa! These bhikṣus long ago resolved upon the Great Vehicle, but they forgot their aspiration along the way. How could you teach them the Lesser Vehicle Dharma? I consider the wisdom of Lesser Vehicle followers to be insignificant and superficial. They are like blind people, unable to discern whether the faculties of living beings are sharp or dull.'

"Then Vimalakīrti entered samādhi and made the bhikṣus aware of their past lives: how they had planted virtuous roots in the presence of five hundred Buddhas and dedicated the merit to the realization of anuttarā samyaksaṃbodhi. Thereupon their minds suddenly opened, and they awakened to their original resolve. The bhikṣus bowed their heads at Vimalakīrti's feet. Then he taught them the Dharma, ensuring that they would never again retreat from anuttarā samyaksaṃbodhi. I now realize that Śrāvakas, being unable to discern the faculties of living beings, should not teach them the Dharma. Therefore, I am not fit to go and inquire about Vimalakīrti's health."

3.027 Then the Buddha told Mahākātyāyana, "Go visit with Vimalakīrti and inquire about his health."

Kātyāyana told the Buddha, "World Honored One! I am not fit to go and inquire about Vimalakīrti's health. Why not? Once, after the Buddha briefly summarized the essence of the Dharma for the bhikṣus, I elaborated upon his explanations of impermanence, suffering, emptiness, nonself, and ultimate stillness. Then Vimalakīrti approached me and said, 'Kātyāyana! You should not use the mind that comes into being and ceases to be to teach the Dharma of ultimate reality. Kātyāyana! Ultimately, phenomena are not subject to coming into being or ceasing to be. This is the meaning of impermanence. The five skandhas, being empty throughout, are not subject to dependent arising. This is the meaning of suffering. Ultimately, phenomena do not exist. This is the meaning of emptiness. Self and nonself are beyond duality. This is the meaning of nonself. Phenomena do not arise, so they do not cease to be.[20] This is the meaning of ultimate stillness.'

"When Vimalakīrti taught this Dharma, the minds of the bhikṣus were liberated. Therefore, I am not fit to go and inquire about Vimalakīrti's health."

Then the Buddha told Aniruddha, "Go visit with 3.028
Vimalakīrti and inquire about his health."

Aniruddha told the Buddha, "World Honored One! I am not fit to go and inquire about Vimalakīrti's health. Why not? Once, when I was walking in meditation, a brahmā named Adorned Purity, accompanied by ten thousand other gods from the Brahmā heavens, approached me, all of them radiant with pure light. Bowing in reverence, they asked me, 'Aniruddha, how far can you see with your heavenly eye?'

"I told them, 'Humane Ones! I can see the entire trichiliocosm of Śakyamuni's Buddhaland as easily as if it were an āmalaka fruit in the palm of my hand.'

"Then Vimalakīrti approached me and said, 'Aniruddha! When you see with your heavenly eye, is there something seen? Or is there not something seen? If there is something seen, that is no different from the five spiritual powers attained through non-Buddhist practices. If there is not something seen, that is the seeing of the unconditioned. There should not be something seen.'

"World Honored One! I was speechless. When the gods from the Brahmā heavens heard these words, they experienced what they never had before. Thereupon they paid their respects to Vimalakīrti and asked him, 'Who in this world has the true heavenly eye?'

"Vimalakīrti replied, 'The Buddha, the World Honored One, has the true heavenly eye. Constantly in samādhi, he sees all the various Buddhalands; and seeing them, he sees them as one.'

"Then Brahmā Adorned Purity and his retinue of five hundred gods from the Brahmā heavens all resolved upon anuttarā samyaksaṃbodhi, reverently bowed at Vimalakīrti's feet, and immediately vanished. Therefore, I am not fit to go and inquire about Vimalakīrti's health."

3.029 Then the Buddha told Upāli, "Go visit with Vimalakīrti and inquire about his health."

Upāli told the Buddha, "World Honored One! I am not fit to go and inquire about Vimalakīrti's health. Why not? Once, when two bhikṣus had broken the precepts but were too ashamed to ask the Buddha about it, they came to me and said, 'Upāli! We have broken the precepts and are truly ashamed. We dare not ask the Buddha about it. Please dispel our worries and remorse so that we can be free from this transgression.' I then began teaching them according to the Dharma.

"At that time Vimalakīrti approached me and said, 'Upāli! Do not exacerbate these bhikṣus' offenses! Simply remove their transgression; do not afflict them further. Why? The nature of transgression is neither inside, outside, nor in between. As the Buddha said, when the mind is defiled, living beings are defiled; when the mind is pure, living beings are pure. Likewise, the mind is neither inside, outside, nor in between. As the mind is like this, so are transgression and phenomena, which do not depart from true thusness. In the same way, Upāli, when, by virtue of the inherent nature of your mind, you attained liberation, had your mind ever been polluted?'

"'No,' I replied.

"Vimalakīrti said, 'It is the same with the inherent purity of the minds of all living beings. Upāli! False thinking is defilement; the absence of false thinking is purity. Delusion is defilement; the absence of delusion is purity. Attaching to self is defilement; not attaching to self is purity. Upāli! Phenomena come and go without ever remaining, like illusions or a lightning flash. They do not linger or wait for one another, nor do they endure even for the space of a single thought. All phenomena are false perceptions; they are like a dream, like a mirage, like the moon's reflection in water, like an image in a mirror. They come about as the result of false thinking. Those who understand this are called upholders of the vinaya. Those who understand this are said to understand well.'

"Then the two bhikṣus said, 'How supremely wise! Upāli cannot equal this. Although he is foremost in upholding the vinaya, he cannot teach like this.'

"I said to them, 'Except for the Tathāgata, no Śrāvaka or Bodhisattva can command this kind of rapturous eloquence. Such is the effulgence of Vimalakīrti's wisdom.'

"Then the bhikṣus' questions and doubts were cleared away, and they resolved upon anuttarā samyaksaṃbodhi, vowing, 'May every living being attain eloquence like this.'

"Therefore, I am not fit to go and inquire about Vimalakīrti's health."

Then the Buddha told Rāhula, "Go visit with 3.030
Vimalakīrti and inquire about his health."

Rāhula told the Buddha, "World Honored One! I am not fit to go and inquire about Vimalakīrti's health. Why not? Once, when the sons of some elders of Vaiśālī approached me, they reverently bowed to me and asked, 'Rāhula! You, the son of the Buddha, relinquished the throne of a wheel-turning king and left the home life to cultivate the Way. What are the benefits of leaving the home life?'

"Then I taught them, according to the Dharma, the meritorious benefits that result from leaving the home life. At that time Vimalakīrti approached me and said, 'Rāhula! Do not teach the meritorious benefits that result from leaving the home life. Why not? That which produces neither benefit nor merit is leaving the home life. That which is conditioned produces benefit and merit. But leaving the home life is unconditioned; that which is unconditioned does not produce either benefit or merit.

3.031 Rāhula! To leave the home life is to be without
this or that or anything in between.
It is to abandon the sixty-two [wrong] views[21]
and abide in nirvāṇa.
It is what is embraced by the wise and practiced
by the sages.
It is to subdue the hordes of demons, transcend
the five destinies, purify the five eyes, attain
the five powers, and develop the five roots.
It is not to be afflicted by others and to leave
behind all kinds of unwholesomeness.
It is to win over all non-Buddhists and transcend
all provisional designations.
It is to rise up from the mud, to be without
attachment, to be without self or what pertains to a self, to have nothing to grasp at, to
be without disturbance, to rejoice within, to
protect the minds of others, to be attuned to
samādhi, and to free oneself from fault.

"'To be like this is truly to leave the home life.'

"Then Vimalakīrti told the elders' sons, 'While the Proper Dharma prevails in the world, you would all do well to leave the home life together. Why? It is difficult to be born when a Buddha is in the world.'

"The elders' sons said, 'Layman, we have heard the Buddha say that people cannot leave the home life without receiving consent from their parents.'

"Vimalakīrti said, 'Just so! The moment that you resolve upon anuttarā samyaksaṃbodhi is the very moment that you leave the home life and become fully ordained.'

"Then the thirty-two elders' sons all resolved upon anuttarā samyaksaṃbodhi. Therefore, I am not fit to go and inquire about Vimalakīrti's health."

Then the Buddha told Ānanda, "Go visit with 3.032
Vimalakīrti and inquire about his health."

Ānanda told the Buddha, "World Honored One! I am not fit to go and inquire about his health. Why not? Once, when the World Honored One had a minor illness and needed cow's milk, I took my bowl and went to the door of a great brāhmaṇa's house. At that time Vimalakīrti approached me and said, 'Ānanda! What are you doing here with your bowl so early in the morning?'

"I told him, 'Layman, I am here because the World Honored One has a minor illness and needs cow's milk.'

"Vimalakīrti said, 'Stop, Ānanda! Stop! Do not say such things. The Tathāgata has a body of vajra. He has already cut off everything unwholesome and amassed everything wholesome. How could he fall ill? How could affliction plague him? Return in silence, Ānanda! Do not slander the Tathāgata or let anyone hear you utter such nonsense. Do not let the gods, with their awe-inspiring dignity, or the Bodhisattvas from other pure lands hear such things. Ānanda! A wheel-turning sage king, though his merit be so little, does not fall ill. How could the Tathāgata, whose limitless merit and wisdom are superior by far, fall ill? Go, Ānanda! Do not bring such disgrace upon us. If non-Buddhists or brāhmins hear this, they will think, "How can such a person be called a teacher? He cannot even cure himself, so how can he cure others?" Hurry, slip away! Do not let others hear of this. Ānanda! Know that the Tathāgata's body is the Dharma body, not the body of desire. The Buddha is the World Honored One; he has transcended the three realms. The Buddha's body has no outflows; he has ended them all. The Buddha's body is unconditioned; it is not subject to any destiny. How could a body like this become ill or afflicted?'

"World Honored One! At that time I felt truly ashamed, wondering if I had misheard the Buddha, although I am so close to him. Then I heard a voice from empty space say, 'Ānanda! It is just as the layman says. The Buddha appears in the troubled world of the five turbidities only for the sake of bringing living beings to liberation; therefore, he employs [skillful] means such as this.[22] Go, Ānanda! Take this milk without shame.' World Honored One! Vimalakīrti has wisdom and eloquence like this. Therefore, I am not fit to go and inquire about Vimalakīrti's health."

Every one of the five hundred great disciples described to the Buddha their own past experience, relating what Vimalakīrti had said to them. And each one told the Buddha, "I am not fit to go and inquire about Vimalakīrti's health."

BODHISATTVAS

CHAPTER 4

Then the Buddha told Maitreya Bodhisattva, "Go visit with Vimalakīrti and inquire about his health."

Maitreya told the Buddha, "World Honored One! I am not fit to go and inquire about his health. Why not? Once, when I was teaching the king of the Tuṣita Heaven and his retinue the practices of irreversibility, Vimalakīrti came to me and said, 'Maitreya! The World Honored One gave you, Humane One, a prediction that you will attain anuttarā samyaksaṃbodhi within a single lifetime. In which lifetime did you receive this prediction? In the past, in the future, or in the present? If in a past life, then it has already passed; if in a future life, then it has not yet arrived; if in the present life, then it will not remain. As the Buddha said, "Bhikṣus! At this very moment, you are born, you grow old, and you die."

"'Suppose the prediction was received in the state 4.033
not subject to coming into being. The state not subject to coming into being is just ultimate reality,[23] in which there is neither the receiving of a prediction nor the attainment of

anuttarā samyaksaṃbodhi. Then how could you, Maitreya, receive the prediction that you will attain anuttarā samyaksaṃbodhi within a single lifetime? Does your prediction result from the coming into being of true thusness? Does your prediction result from the ceasing to be of true thusness? Suppose your prediction results from the coming into being of true thusness. But true thusness does not come into being. Suppose your prediction results from the ceasing to be of true thusness. But true thusness does not cease to be. Living beings are not apart from thusness. Phenomena are not apart from thusness. Sages and worthies are not apart from thusness. Even you, Maitreya, are not apart from thusness. If you, Maitreya, have received a prediction, then all living beings should also receive predictions. Why? Because thusness is free from duality and distinctions. If you, Maitreya, are to attain anuttarā samyaksaṃbodhi, then all living beings should also attain it. Why? Not even a single living being is apart from bodhi. If you, Maitreya, are to realize nirvāṇa, then all living beings should also realize nirvāṇa. Why? The Buddhas know that living beings are inherently tranquil and still, and that that itself is nirvāṇa; there is no other nirvāṇa. Therefore, Maitreya, do not seek to inspire the gods with this Dharma. In reality, there is no such thing as resolving upon anuttarā samyaksaṃbodhi or retreating from it.

4.034 "'Maitreya, you should lead these gods to relinquish any views that make distinctions regarding bodhi. Why? Bodhi cannot be attained with the body, nor can it be attained with the mind.

> Ultimate stillness is bodhi because all characteristics are brought to stillness.
> The absence of contemplation is bodhi because of the transcendence of all conditions.

The cessation of action is bodhi because all thought is brought to an end.
The severing of views is bodhi because of the abandonment of all views.
Transcendence is bodhi because all discursive thought is left behind.
Obstruction is bodhi because of the obstruction of all desires.
The absence of perception is bodhi because greed and attachment are emptied.

Accordance is bodhi because of accordance with thusness. 4.035
Endurance is bodhi because of the enduring nature of all phenomena.
Arriving is bodhi because of arrival at ultimate reality.
Nonduality is bodhi because of the transcendence of mind and mental objects.
Equality is bodhi because of resemblance to empty space.
The unconditioned is bodhi because of the transcendence of arising, abiding, and ceasing to be.
Understanding is bodhi because of the comprehension of living beings' mental activities.
The transcendence of sensory contact is bodhi because the [six sense] gates do not come into contact [with their objects].

Nonengagement is bodhi because all afflictive habitual energy is left behind.
The absence of physical manifestation is bodhi because form and appearance do not exist.

Provisional designations are bodhi because names do not exist.
That which is like an illusion is bodhi because nothing is clung to or abandoned.
Nondisturbance is bodhi because of constant tranquility.
Wholesome stillness is bodhi because its nature is inherently pure.
Nongrasping is bodhi because there is no climbing on conditions.
Nondiscrimination is bodhi because all phenomena are fundamentally equal.
The incomparable is bodhi because nothing can be likened to it.
The subtle and wonderful is bodhi because phenomena are difficult to comprehend.'

"World Honored One! When Vimalakīrti taught this Dharma, two hundred gods realized the patient acceptance of the nonarising of phenomena. Therefore, I am not fit to go and inquire about Vimalakīrti's health."

4.036 Then the Buddha told Youth Radiant Splendor, "Go visit with Vimalakīrti and inquire about his health."

Youth Radiant Splendor told the Buddha, "World Honored One! I am not fit to go and inquire about his health. Why not? Once, as I was about to leave the great city of Vaiśālī, Vimalakīrti had just entered the city. At that time I paid him my respects and asked him, 'Layman, where are you coming from?'

"He said to me, 'I am coming from the place of practice.'

"I asked him, 'What do you mean by the place of practice?'

"He replied,

'A straight mind is the place of practice because
there is nothing false in it.
Practice itself is the place of practice because it
brings things to completion.
A profound resolve is the place of practice
because it causes meritorious virtue to grow.
The bodhi resolve is the place of practice because
it does not go astray.

Giving is the place of practice because there is no
thought of reward.
Upholding precepts is the place of practice
because it fulfills vows.
Patience is the place of practice because it
dissolves all conflict with living beings.
Vigor is the place of practice because it is
without laxity or retreat.
Dhyāna is the place of practice because it makes
the mind supple and wieldy.
Wisdom is the place of practice because it
illuminates all phenomena.

Kindness is the place of practice because it 4.037
regards all living beings equally.
Compassion is the place of practice because it
endures fatigue and suffering.
Joy is the place of practice because it delights in
all Dharmas.
Equanimity is the place of practice because it
puts an end to hatred and love.
Spiritual power is the place of practice because it
perfects the six spiritual powers.
Liberation is the place of practice because desire
is relinquished.

Skillful means are the place of practice because living beings are taught and transformed.

The four methods of attraction are the place of practice because they gather in living beings.
Erudition is the place of practice because what is heard is put into practice.
A pacified mind is the place of practice because it contemplates all phenomena in the appropriate way.
The thirty-seven factors of awakening are the place of practice because conditioned phenomena are relinquished.
The four noble truths are the place of practice because they do not deceive the world.
Dependent arising is the place of practice because ignorance and so on, up to and including old age and death, are endless.
Afflictions are the place of practice because they lead to the understanding of ultimate reality.

4.038 Living beings are the place of practice because they lead to the understanding of nonself.
All phenomena are the place of practice because they lead to the understanding of the emptiness of all phenomena.
Subduing demons is the place of practice because one remains unmoved.
The three realms are the place of practice because one does not take rebirth therein.
The lion's roar is the place of practice because it is fearless.
The [ten] powers, [the four kinds of] fearlessness, and the [eighteen] attributes unique to a

Buddha are the place of practice because they are flawless.
The three spiritual insights are the place of practice because there are no further obstructions.
Knowing all phenomena in a single thought is the place of practice because it brings about the realization of omniscient wisdom.

"'Good man! If Bodhisattvas, having brought themselves into accord with the pāramitās, teach living beings in this way, then you should know that everything they do, even the lifting up and lowering of their feet, comes from the place of practice and is anchored in the Buddhadharma.'

"When Vimalakīrti said this, five hundred gods and humans brought forth the resolve for anuttarā samyaksaṃbodhi. Therefore, I am not fit to go and inquire about Vimalakīrti's health."

Then the Buddha told Bodhisattva Upholding the World, "Go visit with Vimalakīrti and inquire about his health." 4.039

Bodhisattva Upholding the World told the Buddha, "World Honored One! I am not fit to go and inquire about Vimalakīrti's health. Why not? Once, when I was sitting in a quiet room, Pāpīyān, the demon king, came to me in the guise of Śakra, with a retinue of twelve thousand goddesses beating drums and singing to heavenly music. Together with his followers, he bowed at my feet, put his palms together in veneration, and stood to one side. Thinking he was Śakra, I said to him, 'Welcome, Kauśika! Although you may enjoy your blessings, you should not indulge yourself. Contemplate the five desires as impermanent and seek what is fundamentally good; with body, life, and wealth, cultivate what perdures.'[24]

"He then said to me, 'Noble one! Please accept these twelve thousand goddesses, who can clean for you.'

"I replied, 'Kauśika! Do not offer me that which goes against the Dharma. As a śramaṇa, it would be inappropriate for me to accept.'

"Before I could finish what I was saying, Vimalakīrti appeared and said to me, 'This is not Śakra but a demon who has come to vex you!' He then said to the demon, 'You may offer these women to me. A layman like me can accept them.'

"Frightened, the demon thought to himself, 'Vimalakīrti, would you please leave me alone?' He wanted to vanish but was unable to. Try as he might, he could not escape even with all of his spiritual powers.

"At that time a voice from space said, 'Pāpīyān! Give him the women and you may depart.' Terrified, the demon straightaway gave the women to Vimalakīrti.

4.040 "Then Vimalakīrti said to the women, 'This demon has given you to me. You should now bring forth the resolve for anuttarā samyaksaṃbodhi.'

"And he spoke Dharma appropriate to them, inspiring them to bring forth the bodhi resolve. Then he said, 'You have all brought forth the bodhi resolve. Now that you can delight yourselves with joy in the Dharma, you should never again take pleasure in the five desires.'

"The goddesses asked, 'What do you mean by joy in the Dharma?'

"He replied,

'To rejoice in always having faith in the Buddha.
To rejoice in wishing to hear the Dharma.
To rejoice in making offerings to the Sangha.

To rejoice in leaving behind the five desires.
To rejoice in regarding the five skandhas
as thieves.

To rejoice in regarding the four elements as
venomous snakes.
To rejoice in regarding the internal sense bases
as an empty assemblage.
To rejoice in guarding the bodhi resolve.
To rejoice in benefiting living beings.
To rejoice in honoring and making offerings to
teachers.

To rejoice in extensive giving.
To rejoice in rigorous observation of the
precepts.
To rejoice in patience and gentleness.
To rejoice in diligent accumulation of good roots.
To rejoice in dhyāna concentration.
To rejoice in abandoning defilement and
realizing wisdom.

To rejoice in broadening the bodhi resolve. 4.041
To rejoice in quelling the hordes of demons.
To rejoice in severing every affliction.
To rejoice in purifying Buddhalands.
To rejoice in cultivating merit and virtue in
order to perfect the hallmarks.
To rejoice in adorning the site of awakening.
To rejoice in hearing profound Dharma
without fear.

To rejoice in the three doors of liberation
without rejoicing prematurely.[25]
To rejoice in drawing near to fellow cultivators;
and in regard to those who are not fellow
cultivators, to rejoice in bringing forth a
heart free from anger.
To rejoice in protecting bad spiritual teachers.

To rejoice in drawing near to good spiritual
teachers.
To rejoice in the mind that delights in purity.
To rejoice in cultivating countless factors of
awakening.
Such is the Bodhisattva's joy in the Dharma.'

"Then Pāpīyān told the goddesses, 'I want you to return with me to my heavenly palace.'

"They replied, 'You have already given us to this layman. Exulting in the joy of the Dharma, we no longer relish the pleasures of the five desires.'

"The demon said, 'Layman, will you relinquish these women? Those who give everything they own to others are Bodhisattvas.'

"Vimalakīrti replied, 'I have already relinquished them. You may take them with you so that living beings may be led to fulfill their aspirations for the Dharma.'

"Then the goddesses asked Vimalakīrti, 'What should we do after we have returned to the demon's palace?'

4.042 "Vimalakīrti replied, 'Sisters, there is a Dharma-door called the inexhaustible lamp that you must learn. This inexhaustible lamp is like a single lamp that lights a hundred thousand lamps; it lights up the darkness, yet its light is never exhausted. In the same way, sisters, a single Bodhisattva may guide hundreds of thousands of living beings and inspire them to bring forth the resolve for anuttarā samyaksaṃbodhi without ever exhausting his own resolve. As he teaches the Dharma in accordance with conditions, his goodness naturally increases. This is called the inexhaustible lamp. Although you reside in the demon's palace, with this inexhaustible lamp, you can inspire numberless gods and goddesses to bring forth the resolve for anuttarā samyaksaṃbodhi. In this way, you repay the Buddhas' kindness and greatly benefit every living being.'

"At that time the goddesses all bowed at Vimalakīrti's feet; then, following the demon to his palace, they all suddenly vanished. World Honored One! Vimalakīrti's spiritual powers of self-mastery, wisdom, and eloquence are like this. Therefore, I am not fit to go and inquire about his health."

Then the Buddha told the elder's son Wholesome Virtue, "Go visit with Vimalakīrti and inquire about his health." 4.043

Wholesome Virtue told the Buddha, "World Honored One! I am not fit to go and inquire about his health. Why not? Once, at my father's, I was hosting a great assembly of almsgiving for śramaṇas, brāhmaṇas, all kinds of non-Buddhists, the poor, the lowly, the lonely and bereft, and beggars. This went on for seven days. Then Vimalakīrti came to the assembly and said to me, 'Elder's son! You should not have conducted this great assembly of almsgiving in this way. It should be an assembly for the giving of Dharma. What use is an assembly for the giving of wealth?'

"I replied, 'Layman! What is an assembly for the giving of Dharma?'

"He replied, 'This kind of assembly transcends time; in a single instant, the Dharma is given to all living beings. This is called an assembly for the giving of Dharma.'

"I said, 'What does that mean?'

"He replied,

'In order to realize bodhi, you bring forth a heart of kindness.
In order to rescue living beings, you bring forth a heart of great compassion.
In order to uphold the Proper Dharma, you bring forth a heart of joy.
In order to gather in wisdom, you bring forth a heart of equanimity.

In order to counteract stinginess, you practice dāna pāramitā.
In order to transform transgression, you practice śīla pāramitā.
In order to realize nonself, you practice kṣānti pāramitā.
In order to free yourself from body and mind, you practice vīrya pāramitā.
In order to cultivate stillness,[26] you practice dhyāna pāramitā.
In order to cultivate omniscient wisdom, you practice prajñā pāramitā.

4.044 In teaching living beings, you cultivate emptiness.
Without forsaking the conditioned, you empty all characteristics.
In manifesting birth, nothing is done.
In protecting the Proper Dharma, you exercise the power of skillful means.
In order to save living beings, you employ the four methods of attraction.
In order to serve everyone with respect, you rid yourself of pride.
With regard to body, life, and wealth, you cultivate what perdures.[27]

In practicing the six types of mindfulness, you uphold proper mindfulness.
In practicing the six ways of maintaining harmony,[28] you develop an honest mind.
In properly cultivating wholesome deeds, you practice a pure livelihood.
With a pure and joyful mind, you draw near to sages and worthies.

In abandoning aversion toward those who do
evil, you subdue your mind.
In leaving the home life, you deepen your resolve.
In practicing as instructed, you acquire great
learning.
In freeing yourself from contention, you
establish a place of seclusion.
Turning toward the Buddhas' wisdom, you sit
in stillness.

In freeing living beings from their bonds, you 4.045
establish the ground of cultivation.
In order to perfect the hallmarks and purify
the Buddhalands, you cultivate meritorious
deeds.
In comprehending the thoughts of living beings
and teaching the Dharma appropriate to
them, you cultivate wisdom.
In comprehending all phenomena without grasping
or rejecting, you cultivate knowledge and
enter the door of thusness.
In putting an end to all afflictions, all obstacles,
and all unwholesomeness, you practice all
wholesome deeds.
In order to realize omniscient wisdom and all
wholesome practices, you cultivate the aids
to the Path leading to Buddhahood.

"'This, good man, is an assembly for the giving of Dharma. If Bodhisattvas host an assembly for the giving of Dharma in this way, then they are great donors and fields of blessings for the world.'

"World Honored One, when Vimalakīrti taught this Dharma, two hundred people from the multitude of brāhmaṇas brought forth the resolve for anuttarā samyaksaṃbodhi. My mind attained a purity I had never known before. I bowed my head to the ground at Vimalakīrti's feet. Right then I removed my jeweled necklace, worth hundreds of thousands [of ounces of gold], and offered it to him, but he refused to accept it. I urged him, 'Layman, please accept this necklace and do with it whatever you wish.'

4.046 "Then Vimalakīrti took the jeweled necklace and divided it in two. He offered one half to the lowliest beggars among the multitude and gave the other to Tathāgata Difficult to Conquer. Everyone in the assembly saw this Tathāgata Difficult to Conquer, who lives in the Land of Brilliance. In the air above that Buddha, they saw the necklace transform into a jeweled platform of four pillars splendidly adorned on all sides with adornments that did not obstruct one another. Then, having displayed these spiritual transformations, Vimalakīrti said, 'If a donor can give impartially to the lowliest beggar—just as the Tathāgata, who is a field of blessings, impartially bestows great compassion without distinction, seeking no reward in return—this is called the perfection of the giving of Dharma.'

"One of the lowliest beggars in the city, hearing what Vimalakīrti had said and witnessing his spiritual power, brought forth the resolve for anuttarā samyaksaṃbodhi. Therefore, I am not fit to go and inquire about his health."

Every one of the Bodhisattvas described to the Buddha their own past experience, relating what Vimalakīrti had said to them. And each one told the Buddha, "I am not fit to go and inquire about Vimalakīrti's health."

MAÑJUŚRĪ INQUIRES ABOUT VIMALAKĪRTI'S HEALTH

CHAPTER 5

Then the Buddha told Mañjuśrī, "Go visit with Vimalakīrti and inquire about his health."

Mañjuśrī said to the Buddha, "World Honored One! That venerable person is not easy to equal in conversation. He profoundly comprehends the essence of things as they really are. Skillfully teaching the essentials of the Dharma, he is unimpeded in his eloquence and unobstructed in his wisdom. He has mastered all the conduct of a Bodhisattva; and of the Buddhas' esoteric treasuries, there is not one he cannot enter. He subdues the hordes of demons, roams around playfully with his spiritual powers, and has brought his wisdom and skillful means to perfection. Even so, I shall obey the Buddha's sagely decree and go inquire about his health."

Then the Bodhisattvas, Śrāvakas, Śakyas, brahmās, four heavenly kings, and the rest of the assembly all thought, "Today two Great Beings, Mañjuśrī and Vimalakīrti, will talk together. What they say will surely be wonderful Dharma!" So eight thousand Bodhisattvas, five hundred Śravakas, and hundreds of thousands of gods all wished to go along. Thereupon Mañjuśrī, surrounded respectfully by all these Bodhisattvas, Śrāvakas, and gods, entered the city of Vaiśali.

5.047 At that time the elder Vimalakīrti thought, "Mañjuśrī and the great assembly are on their way!" Then, by means of his spiritual powers, he removed everything from his room, including his attendants. Only his bed remained, on which he lay as though ill.

Arriving there, Mañjuśrī saw that the room was empty. There was only Vimalakīrti lying on the bed. Vimalakīrti said, "Welcome, Mañjuśrī! Your coming is not coming. Our seeing each other is not seeing."

Mañjuśrī replied, "So it is, layman! If one has come, there is no more coming. If one has gone, there is no more going. Why is that? That which comes, comes from nowhere; that which goes, goes nowhere. That which can be seen cannot be seen further. Leave it at that, layman! Is your illness bearable? Has treatment improved your condition or prevented it from worsening? The World Honored One has made countless earnest inquiries about you: How did your illness come about? How long have you been sick? How can your illness be brought to an end?"

Vimalakīrti said, "From ignorance, craving arises; then sickness appears. I am sick because living beings are sick. If their sickness went away, mine would also disappear. Why is this? For the sake of living beings, Bodhisattvas enter the cycle of birth and death. Where there is birth and death, there is sickness. If living beings can be without sickness, then Bodhisattvas will never be sick again. Consider a couple with a single child: if the child gets sick, the parents also get sick; if he recovers, the parents also recover. Bodhisattvas are like this. They love living beings as if they were their own children. When living beings are sick, Bodhisattvas are also sick; when living beings recover, Bodhisattvas also recover. What is the cause of their sickness? The sickness of Bodhisattvas comes from great compassion."

Mañjuśrī asked, "Layman, why is your room empty 5.048
of attendants?"

Vimalakīrti replied, "The lands of all Buddhas are also empty."

Mañjuśrī said, "What makes them empty?"

Vimalakīrti replied, "Emptiness empties them."

Mañjuśrī said, "Can emptiness be emptied?"

Vimalakīrti replied, "When the discrimination of emptiness is absent, there is emptiness."

Mañjuśrī said, "Can emptiness be discriminated?"

Vimalakīrti replied, "Discrimination is also empty."

Mañjuśrī said, "Where can emptiness be found?"

Vimalakīrti replied, "In the sixty-two [wrong] views."

Mañjuśrī said, "Where can the sixty-two [wrong] views be found?"

Vimalakīrti replied, "In the liberation of all Buddhas."

Mañjuśrī said, "Where can the liberation of all Buddhas be found?"

Vimalakīrti replied, "Right within the minds of living beings. Earlier, the Humane One wanted to know, 'Where are your attendants?' All demons and unorthodox practitioners are my attendants. Why is that? Demons delight in birth and death, and Bodhisattvas do not renounce birth and death. Unorthodox practitioners delight in erroneous views, and Bodhisattvas are unmoved by such views."

Mañjuśrī said, "What are the characteristics of your illness?"

Vimalakīrti replied, "My illness is formless and invisible."

5.049 Mañjuśrī said, "Is your illness physical or mental?"

Vimalakīrti replied, "My illness is not physical, for I transcend physical form. Nor is it mental, for the mind is an illusion."

Mañjuśrī said, "Of the four great elements—earth, water, fire, and wind—to which does your illness belong?"

Vimalakīrti replied, "It is not an illness of the earth element, nor is it apart from the earth element. The same is true of water, fire, and wind. However, the sickness of all beings arises from the four great elements. And because they are sick, I am sick."

Then Mañjuśrī Bodhisattva asked Vimalakīrti, "How should a Bodhisattva comfort Bodhisattvas who are sick?"

Vimalakīrti replied, "Teach them that, although the body is impermanent, they should not feel disgust toward it; although the body undergoes suffering, they should take no delight in nirvāṇa; although the body is without intrinsic essence, they should guide and teach living beings nonetheless; although the body is empty and still, they should not seek ultimate stillness; although they repent of previous wrongs, they should relinquish the notion of the past. Through their own sickness, they can sympathize with the sickness of others. Understanding the suffering of numberless eons, they should now set their minds on benefiting living beings. They should recollect the merit that they have cultivated and dedicate themselves to leading a pure life. They should not give rise to worry or distress; instead, they should constantly advance with vigor. They should become physician kings who remedy all sickness. A Bodhisattva should comfort sick Bodhisattvas in this way, and thereby bring them joy."

Mañjuśrī asked, "Layman, how should Bodhisattvas who are sick regulate their minds?"

5.050 Vimalakīrti said, "Bodhisattvas who are sick should reflect as follows: 'My present illness is the result of the delusion, distortion, and many other afflictions I experienced in previous lives. But this illness has no essential existence, so how could I get sick? Why do I say this? The four elements aggregate into what is conventionally called a "body." The four elements have no inherent nature, and the body has no intrinsic essence. Moreover, sickness comes about from attachment to a self. Therefore, I should not become attached to a self.' Understanding the origin of illness, one does away with the conceptions of self and living beings. In contemplating phenomena, one should reflect as follows: 'This body is merely the coming together of myriad phenomena. When those phenomena arise, it arises; when those phenomena cease, it ceases. Lacking the knowledge of others, when these phenomena arise, they cannot say to one another, "I am arising"; when they cease, they cannot say to one another, "I am ceasing."'

"Then, in order to do away with the thought of phe- 5.051
nomena, Bodhisattvas who are sick should reflect as follows: 'Such notions of phenomena are also upside down. I should leave them behind, for they are a source of grave troubles.' How does one leave them behind? By leaving behind the self and what pertains to the self. How does one leave behind the self and what pertains to the self? By transcending duality. How does one transcend duality? By not regarding phenomena as internal or external and instead practicing impartiality. What is meant by impartiality? When self and nirvāṇa are the same.

"Why? Both self and nirvāṇa are empty. In what way are they empty? They are nothing but names. These two have no fixed essence. Those who realize this impartiality have no sickness other than [their attachment to] emptiness—and even that sickness is empty. Therefore, by means of the freedom from perception, Bodhisattvas who are sick perceive all that there is to perceive. Although they have not realized Buddhahood, they do not seek realization through the cessation of perception.

5.052 "When the Bodhisattva experiences suffering of the body, he should recall beings in the lower destinies and bring forth a mind of great compassion: 'As I am regulated, I regulate all living beings. I only get rid of the sickness, not the phenomena. I teach and guide them to eliminate the source of their sickness. What is the source of their sickness? Grasping is the source of their sickness. What is grasped? The three realms. How can they put an end to their grasping? When they let go of attaining. When there is nothing to attain, nothing can be grasped. What is meant by letting go of attaining? To transcend dualistic views. What are dualistic views? The internal and the external, neither of which can be grasped.'

"Mañjuśrī, this is how a Bodhisattva who is sick regulates his mind. He does this in order to put an end to the suffering caused by old age, sickness, and death. This is the Bodhisattva's bodhi. If a Bodhisattva does not cultivate in this way, then his efforts will not bring about benefit. Just as one who overcomes his enemies can be called a hero, those who overcome old age, sickness, and death can be called Bodhisattvas.

"Furthermore, Bodhisattvas who are sick should think, 'Just as my sickness is illusory and insubstantial, the sickness of living beings is also illusory and insubstantial.' If, while contemplating in this way, they bring forth great compassion on the basis of affection, they should let it go. Why? Bodhisattvas bring forth great compassion by cutting off the guest dust of afflictions. Those whose compassion arises from affection will grow weary of birth and death. Those who renounce affection will not feel this kind of weariness; no matter where they are born, they will not be blinded by such affection. Those Bodhisattvas who can free themselves from the fetters of birth [and death] can teach living beings to free themselves from their fetters. As the Buddha said, 'Those who are fettered cannot free others from their fetters. Only those who have unfettered themselves can liberate others.' Therefore, Bodhisattvas should not fetter themselves.

"What are fetters? What is liberation? Clinging to 5.053
the flavor of dhyāna is the Bodhisattva's fetter. The expedient of taking rebirth is the Bodhisattva's liberation. Without skillful means, wisdom is a fetter; with skillful means, wisdom brings about liberation. Without wisdom, skillful means are a fetter; with wisdom, skillful means bring about liberation.

"What does it mean to say that without skillful means, wisdom is a fetter? Suppose that, although Bodhisattvas adorn the Buddhalands, bring living beings to perfection, and regulate themselves by means of emptiness, marklessness, and effortlessness, they do so with affection. This is when, without skillful means, wisdom is a fetter.

"What does it mean to say that with skillful means, wisdom brings about liberation? Suppose that Bodhisattvas, without affection, adorn the Buddhalands, bring living beings to perfection, and regulate themselves by means of emptiness, marklessness, and effortlessness—and thereby do not grow weary. This is when, with skillful means, wisdom brings about liberation.

"What does it mean to say that without wisdom, 5.054
skillful means are a fetter? Suppose that Bodhisattvas seek to plant many roots of virtue but have yet to let go of afflictions like greed, anger, and wrong views. This is when, without wisdom, skillful means are a fetter.

"What does it mean to say that with wisdom, skillful means bring about liberation? Suppose that, in planting many roots of virtue, Bodhisattvas have already let go of afflictions like greed, anger, and wrong views; and with these roots, they make dedications to the realization of anuttarā samyaksaṃbodhi. This is when, with wisdom, skillful means bring about liberation.

"Mañjuśrī, Bodhisattvas who are sick should contemplate all phenomena in this way.

"Moreover, Bodhisattvas should regard the body as impermanent, a mass of suffering, empty, and without self. This is wisdom. Although the body is sick, Bodhisattvas, remaining constantly in the cycle of birth and death, benefit all without ever growing weary. This is skillful means.

"Furthermore, Bodhisattvas should regard the body as inseparable from sickness and sickness as inseparable from the body. Sickness and the body are one: neither comes before the other; neither comes after. This is wisdom. Although the body is subject to sickness, Bodhisattvas do not seek eternal stillness. This is skillful means.

"Mañjuśrī, Bodhisattvas who are sick regulate their minds in this way: they do not abide in regulation, nor do they abide in nonregulation. Why not? To abide in nonregulation is the way of the foolish. To abide in regulation is the way of the Śrāvakas. Therefore, Bodhisattvas should not abide in regulation or nonregulation. To be apart from these two is Bodhisattva practice.

5.055 In the midst of birth and death, they are free of
defilement; though dwelling in nirvāṇa,
they do not enter eternal stillness: this is
Bodhisattva practice.
That which is neither the practice of ordinary
people nor the practice of sages and
worthies: this is Bodhisattva practice.
That which is neither a defiled practice nor a
pure practice: this is Bodhisattva practice.

Although they are no longer subject to the influence of demons, they appear to subdue the host of demons: this is Bodhisattva practice.
They seek omniscient wisdom but avoid premature realization:[29] this is Bodhisattva practice.

Although they understand all phenomena as nonarising, they defer the attainment of realization: this is Bodhisattva practice.
Although they contemplate the twelve links of dependent arising, they appear to hold wrong views: this is Bodhisattva practice.
Although they gather in all living beings, they are free from affection: this is Bodhisattva practice.
Although they delight in withdrawal, they do not regard the cessation of body and mind as ultimate stillness: this is Bodhisattva practice.
Although they remain in the three realms, they do not disrupt the inherent nature of all phenomena: this is Bodhisattva practice.

Although in the midst of emptiness, they plant myriad roots of virtue: this is Bodhisattva practice. 5.056
Although they practice marklessness, they rescue living beings: this is Bodhisattva practice.
Although they practice effortlessness, they appear to take rebirth: this is Bodhisattva practice.

Although they practice nonarising, they
engage in all wholesome practices: this is
Bodhisattva practice.
Although they practice the six pāramitās, they
know the minds and thoughts of every living
being: this is Bodhisattva practice.
Although they practice the six spiritual powers,
they do not completely end their outflows:
this is Bodhisattva practice.
Although they practice the four infinite states of
mind, they are not attached to rebirth in the
Brahmā realm: this is Bodhisattva practice.
Although they practice dhyāna, liberation, and
samādhi, they do not take rebirth on the
basis of their meditative attainment: this is
Bodhisattva practice.

5.057 Although they practice the four foundations
of mindfulness, they do not forever leave
behind the body, sense perception, mind, or
phenomena: this is Bodhisattva practice.
Although they practice the four kinds of right
effort, they do not abandon vigor in body and
mind: this is Bodhisattva practice.
Although they practice the four steps to spiritual
powers, they also attain spiritual powers of
self-mastery: this is Bodhisattva practice.
Although they cultivate the five roots, they also
discern the keen and dull faculties of living
beings: this is Bodhisattva practice.
Although they practice the five powers, they joy-
fully aspire to attain the Buddhas' ten pow-
ers: this is Bodhisattva practice.
Although they practice the seven factors of
awakening, they set their minds on the

Buddhas' wisdom: this is Bodhisattva practice.
Although they practice the eightfold path, they delight in walking the Buddhas' boundless Path: this is Bodhisattva practice.

Although they practice calming and contemplation as aids to the Path, they are not carried along into ultimate stillness: this is Bodhisattva practice. 5.058
Although they understand that phenomena do not come into being or cease to be, they adorn their bodies with hallmarks: this is Bodhisattva practice.
Although they appear as Śrāvakas and Pratyekabuddhas, they do not forsake the Buddhas' Dharma: this is Bodhisattva practice.
Although they accord with the ultimate purity of all phenomena, they manifest in different bodies in response to various conditions: this is Bodhisattva practice.
Although they regard all Buddhalands as eternally still like empty space, they manifest many kinds of pure Buddhalands: this is Bodhisattva practice.
Although they realize Buddhahood, turn the Dharma wheel, and enter nirvāṇa, they do not abandon the Bodhisattva Path: this is Bodhisattva practice."

When Vimalakīrti said this, eight thousand gods in the great assembly led by Mañjuśrī brought forth the resolve for anuttarā samyaksaṃbodhi.

THE INCONCEIVABLE

CHAPTER 6

At that time Śāriputra, seeing that there were no seats in Vimalakīrti's room, thought to himself, "Where is this assembly of Bodhisattvas and Śrāvakas going to sit?"

The elder Vimalakīrti, knowing Śāriputra's thoughts, said to him, "Humane One, do you come for the Dharma or for a seat?"

Śāriputra said, "I come for the Dharma, not for a seat."

Vimalakīrti said, "Just so, Śāriputra! Those who seek the Dharma do not care even about their bodies or lives, how much the less a seat. Those who seek the Dharma do not seek form, sense perception, cognition, mental formations, or consciousness. They do not seek the sense realms or sense fields, nor do they seek the realms of desire, form, or the formless.

"Śāriputra! Those who seek the Dharma free them- 6.059
selves from attachment to the Buddha, Dharma, and Sangha. Those who seek the Dharma do not seek the acknowledgement

of suffering, do not seek the severance of the cause of suffering, do not aspire to the end of suffering, and do not cultivate the Path. Why? The Dharma is free of sophistry. If I say that I must acknowledge suffering, sever the cause of suffering, aspire to end suffering, and cultivate the Path, I am not seeking the Dharma, I am engaging in sophistry.

6.060 Śāriputra! The Dharma is tranquil and still. If you practice that which comes into being and ceases to be, you are not seeking the Dharma, you are seeking that which comes into being and ceases to be.

The Dharma is free of greed. If you become greedy for the Dharma or even nirvāṇa, you are not seeking the Dharma, you are being greedy.

The Dharma is independent of phenomena. If you interact with phenomena, you are not seeking the Dharma, you are interacting with phenomena.

The Dharma cannot be grasped or relinquished. If you grasp or relinquish the Dharma, you are not seeking the Dharma, you are grasping or relinquishing.

The Dharma does not abide anywhere. If there is anywhere to abide, this is not seeking the Dharma, this is attachment.

The Dharma is free from characteristics. If you understand the Dharma by means of characteristics, you are not seeking the Dharma, you are seeking characteristics.

The Dharma cannot be depended upon. If you depend upon the Dharma, you are not seeking the Dharma, you are fixing your mind on the Dharma.

The Dharma cannot be seen, heard, felt, or perceived. If you see, hear, feel, or perceive the Dharma, you are not seeking the Dharma, you are seeing, hearing, feeling, and perceiving.

The Dharma is unconditioned. If you practice the conditioned, you are not seeking the Dharma, you are seeking the conditioned.

"Therefore Śāriputra, those who seek the Dharma should not seek anything."

When Vimalakīrti said this, five hundred gods 6.061
attained the clarity of the Dharma eye with respect to all phenomena.

Then the elder Vimalakīrti asked Mañjuśrī, "Humane One, you have traveled throughout countless tens of millions of koṭis of asaṃkhyeyas of lands. Which Buddhaland has lion thrones brought about by merit most sublime?"

Mañjuśrī replied, "Layman! To the east, beyond lands as many as the grains of sand in thirty-six Ganges Rivers, there is a world called Sumeru Banner.[30] In that world is a Buddha named Sumeru Lamp King. That Buddha's body is eighty-four thousand yojanas tall. His lion throne is also eighty-four thousand yojanas high and is foremost in adornment."

Then, in a display of spiritual power by the elder Vimalakīrti, that Buddha sent to the elder's room thirty-two thousand lion thrones, broad, lofty, and purely graced. The Bodhisattvas, Śrāvakas, Śakras, brahmās, and four heavenly kings had never seen such a thing before. Vimalakīrti's room expanded to accommodate all thirty-two thousand lion thrones without difficulty. Vaiśālī, Jambudvīpa, and the four great continents were not crowded in any way; all looked the same as before.

6.062 Then Vimalakīrti said to Mañjuśrī, "Take a seat upon a lion throne along with the other Bodhisattvas of superior attainment, and each of you adjust your body to fit the throne."

Those Bodhisattvas of spiritual attainment then transformed themselves to a height of forty-two thousand yojanas and sat upon the lion thrones. But the newly resolved Bodhisattvas and Śrāvakas were unable to climb upon the thrones.

Then Vimalakīrti said to Śāriputra, "Take a seat upon a lion throne."

Śāriputra replied, "Layman! These thrones are too broad and lofty for me to climb onto."

Vimalakīrti said, "Śāriputra! Bow to Tathāgata Sumeru Lamp King and you will be able to sit." The newly resolved Bodhisattvas and Śrāvakas then bowed to Tathāgata Sumeru Lamp King and were able to sit upon the lion thrones.

Śāriputra said, "Layman, this is unprecedented! A room as small as this can accommodate thrones as broad and lofty as these without affecting Vaiśālī or crowding Jambudvīpa's villages and cities or the palaces of the gods, dragon kings, ghosts, and spirits of the four great continents."

6.063 Vimalakīrti replied, "Śāriputra! The Buddhas and Bodhisattvas have a liberation called inconceivable. A Bodhisattva who abides in this liberation can fit the broad and lofty Mount Sumeru within a mustard seed without shrinking one or enlarging the other; Mount Sumeru, the king of mountains, will remain the same size. The gods in the Heaven of the Four Kings and the Trāyastriṃśa Heaven will be completely unaware of where they have been put; only those who are to be saved will see Mount Sumeru inside the mustard seed. This is called abiding in the Dharma-door of inconceivable liberation.

"Moreover, such a Bodhisattva can fit the waters of the four great seas into a single hair pore without disturbing any of the fish, freshwater turtles, sea turtles, crocodiles, or other marine creatures; the seas will remain the same size. The dragons, ghosts, spirits, and asuras will be completely unaware of where they have been put. All these living beings will remain undisturbed.

"Moreover, Śāriputra! A Bodhisattva who abides in the inconceivable liberation can break off the trichiliocosm and take it in his right hand like a potter's wheel, then throw it beyond worlds as many as the grains of sand in the Ganges. The living beings therein will be completely unaware of where they have gone. This Bodhisattva can then return the trichiliocosm to its original place without these living beings thinking that they have traveled and returned; the trichiliocosm will remain the same.

"Moreover, Śāriputra! If there are living beings who 6.064
can be saved through their desire for a long life span, such a Bodhisattva will stretch seven days into an eon so that these living beings will take them for an eon. If there are living beings who can be saved through their desire for a short life span, this Bodhisattva will shrink an eon into seven days so that these living beings will take it for seven days.

"Moreover, Śāriputra! A Bodhisattva who abides in the inconceivable liberation can amass in one land all the adornments of every Buddhaland and show them to living beings. Furthermore, this Bodhisattva can put all the living beings from one Buddhaland in his right hand and show them everything by flying everywhere in the ten directions, without any of them moving from their original place.

"Moreover, Śāriputra! Such a Bodhisattva can make visible in a single hair pore all the offerings made to the Buddhas by living beings in the ten directions. Furthermore, he can make visible in a single hair pore the suns, moons, and stars of all the lands in the ten directions.

"Moreover, Śāriputra! Such a Bodhisattva can draw into his mouth all the winds from the worlds of the ten directions without damaging his body or felling any trees. Furthermore, when the eon ends in a great conflagration that pervades the worlds of the ten directions, he can swallow all the fires into his belly and remain unharmed as they continue to burn.

6.065 "Furthermore, from the worlds below, beyond Buddhalands as many as the grains of sand in the Ganges, such a Bodhisattva can take one Buddhaland and carry it upward to the worlds above, beyond worlds as numberless as the grains of sand in the Ganges, as easily as lifting a jujube leaf on the tip of a needle, without causing the least disturbance.

"Moreover, Śāriputra! Using his spiritual powers, a Bodhisattva who abides in the inconceivable liberation can appear in the body of a Buddha, the body of a Pratyekabuddha, the body of a Śrāvaka, the body of a Śakra, the body of a brahmā, the body of a heavenly king, or the body of a wheel-turning king. Furthermore, he can transform all the sounds from the worlds of the ten directions—whether superior, average, or inferior—into the voice of a Buddha teaching impermanence, suffering, emptiness, and nonself. The various Dharmas taught by Buddhas in the ten directions can also be heard. Śāriputra! I have just briefly described the power of the Bodhisattvas' inconceivable liberation. If I were to describe it extensively to the end of future eons, I would not be able to finish."

6.066 At that time, having heard the Dharma-door of the Bodhisattvas' inconceivable liberation and marveling at this unprecedented occasion, Mahākāśyapa said to Śāriputra, "Suppose someone shows images to a blind person. He will not be able to see them. In the same way, the Śrāvakas who have heard this Dharma-door of inconceivable liberation cannot understand it. Upon hearing this, who among the wise would not bring forth the resolve for anuttarā samyaksaṃbodhi? What have we done to eternally sever our roots, so that we have become sterile seeds in the Great Vehicle? Upon hearing this Dharma-door of inconceivable liberation, all Śrāvakas should weep bitterly, letting their cries reverberate throughout the trichiliocosm, while all Bodhisattvas should rejoice greatly and reverently receive this Dharma. If there is a Bodhisattva with faith and understanding in this Dharma-door of inconceivable liberation, the demonic hordes will not be able to do anything to him."

When Mahākāśyapa said this, thirty-two thousand gods all brought forth the resolve for anuttarā samyaksaṃbodhi.

At that time Vimalakīrti said to Mahākāśyapa, 6.067
"Humane One! Among the countless asaṃkhyeya worlds of the ten directions, many of the demon kings are Bodhisattvas abiding in the inconceivable liberation. By means of the power of skillful means, they appear as demon kings to teach and transform living beings.

"Moreover, Kāśyapa! Countless Bodhisattvas in the ten directions encounter people who ask them for their hands, feet, ears, or nose; their head, eyes, marrow, or brain; their blood, flesh, skin, or bones; their villages, cities, wives, children, servants, or carriages drawn by elephants or horses; their gold, silver, vaiḍūrya, giant clam shell, carnelian, coral, amber, pearl, jade, or cowry; or their clothing or food. Many of these people who come to make requests are Bodhisattvas abiding in the inconceivable liberation. Through the power of skillful means, they come to test these Bodhisattvas and strengthen their resolve. What does that mean? Because Bodhisattvas who abide in the inconceivable liberation have awe-inspiring virtue, they are able to show living beings how difficult the practice of giving is by urging other Bodhisattvas to give. Ordinary beings are lowly, so they do not have the power to urge Bodhisattvas in this way. Likewise, the kicking and stamping of dragons and elephants is beyond what a donkey can do. This is called the skillful Dharma-door of wisdom of Bodhisattvas who abide in the inconceivable liberation."

CONTEMPLATING LIVING BEINGS

CHAPTER 7

At that time Mañjuśrī asked Vimalakīrti, "How should a Bodhisattva contemplate living beings?"

Vimalakīrti replied, "A Bodhisattva should contemplate living beings just as a magician regards the people he conjures. A Bodhisattva should contemplate living beings just as a wise man regards the moon's reflection in water, his face in a mirror, a mirage, an echo, clouds in the sky, a mass of foam, bubbles in water, the solid core of the plantain tree,[31] the permanence of lightning, a fifth great element, a sixth skandha, a seventh sense faculty, a thirteenth sense field, or a nineteenth sense realm. A Bodhisattva should regard living beings in this way. A Bodhisattva should contemplate living beings as being like form in the formless realm, a sprout from a burnt seed, a Srotāpanna [stream-enterer] with a view of self, an Anāgāmin [never-returner] taking rebirth in a womb, an Arhat with the three poisons, a Bodhisattva who has attained patience yet gives rise to craving and anger and transgresses the precepts, a Buddha with habitual afflictions, a blind man who can see form, the presence of breath within the samādhi of cessation of sense perception and cognition, the tracks of a bird's flight in the sky, a sterile woman giving birth, a transformation being giving rise to afflictions, a dream of being awake, the rebirth of someone who has achieved ultimate stillness, and a fire without any smoke. A Bodhisattva should regard living beings in this way."

7.068 Manjuśrī asked, "Having contemplated living beings in this way, how should a Bodhisattva practice kindness?"

Vimalakīrti replied, "Having contemplated living beings in this way, a Bodhisattva then thinks to himself, 'I should teach this Dharma for the sake of living beings.' This is true kindness.

Bodhisattvas practice the kindness of ultimate stillness because nothing comes into being.
Bodhisattvas practice a kindness free of agitation because they are free of affliction.
Bodhisattvas practice impartial kindness because the three periods of time are equal.
Bodhisattvas practice a kindness free of contention because nothing arises.
Bodhisattvas practice the kindness of nonduality because they do not associate with internal or external.
Bodhisattvas practice indestructible kindness because it is ultimately inexhaustible.
Bodhisattvas practice enduring kindness because their mind is unwavering.
Bodhisattvas practice the kindness of purity because of the inherent purity of all phenomena.
Bodhisattvas practice boundless kindness because it is like empty space.

Bodhisattvas practice an Arhat's kindness
because it shatters afflictions.
Bodhisattvas practice a Bodhisattva's kindness 7.069
because it brings harmony to living beings.
Bodhisattvas practice a Tathāgata's kindness
because they realize things as they really are.
Bodhisattvas practice a Buddha's kindness
because it awakens living beings.
Bodhisattvas practice a self-originating kindness
because it is independent of causality.
Bodhisattvas practice the kindness of bodhi
because all kindness has the same flavor.
Bodhisattvas practice a peerless kindness
because they cut off all affection.
Bodhisattvas practice a kindness of great compassion because it leads to the Great Vehicle.
Bodhisattvas practice a tireless kindness
because they contemplate all as empty and without self.

Bodhisattvas practice the kindness of giving the Dharma because there is nothing they cannot forsake. 7.070
Bodhisattvas practice the kindness of upholding precepts because it transforms those who violate precepts.
Bodhisattvas practice the kindness of patience
because it protects self and others.
Bodhisattvas practice the kindness of vigor
because it carries all living beings.
Bodhisattvas practice the kindness of dhyāna meditation because there is no attachment to the flavor [of dhyāna].
Bodhisattvas practice the kindness of wisdom
because it never misses the opportune time.

Bodhisattvas practice the kindness of skillful means because they manifest all.
Bodhisattvas practice a forthright kindness because their hearts are straightforward and pure.
Bodhisattvas practice a kindness of profound resolve because they leave behind extraneous practices.
Bodhisattvas practice a kindness without deception because they are not hypocritical.
Bodhisattvas practice a kindness of peace and joy because all are enabled to attain the bliss of the Buddha.

"Such is the great kindness of a Bodhisattva."

7.071 Then Mañjuśrī asked, "What is compassion?"

Vimālakīrti replied, "Whatever merit the Bodhisattva generates is shared with all living beings."

Mañjuśrī said, "What is joy?"

Vimālakīrti replied, "When benefiting living beings, the Bodhisattva rejoices without regret."

Mañjuśrī said, "What is renunciation?"

Vimālakīrti replied, "When generating merit, the Bodhisattva has no expectations."

Mañjuśrī said, "Fearing transmigration, what should the Bodhisattva rely upon?"

Vimalakīrti replied, "The Bodhisattva, fearing transmigration, should rely upon the power of the Tathāgatas' merit."

Mañjuśrī said, "Wishing to rely upon the power of the Tathāgatas' merit, what should the Bodhisattva abide in?"

Vimalakīrti replied, "The Bodhisattva, wishing to rely upon the power of the Tathāgatas' merit, should abide in the liberation of all living beings."

Mañjuśrī said, "Wishing to liberate all living beings, what should the Bodhisattva put an end to?" 7.072

Vimalakīrti replied, "The Bodhisattva, wishing to liberate all living beings, should put an end to their afflictions."

Mañjuśrī said, "Wishing to put an end to their afflictions, what should the Bodhisattva practice?"

Vimalakīrti replied, "The Bodhisattva should practice proper mindfulness."

Mañjuśrī said, "How should a Bodhisattva practice proper mindfulness?"

Vimalakīrti replied, "The Bodhisattva should practice that which does not come into being or cease to be."

Mañjuśrī said, "Which phenomena do not come into being? Which phenomena do not cease to be?"

Vimalakīrti replied, "That which is unwholesome does not come into being; that which is wholesome does not cease to be."

Mañjuśrī said, "What is the origin of the wholesome and the unwholesome?"

Vimalakīrti replied, "The body is the origin." 7.073

Mañjuśrī said, "What is the origin of the body?"

Vimalakīrti replied, "Desire and greed are the origin."

Mañjuśrī said, "What is the origin of desire and greed?"

Vimalakīrti replied, "False discrimination is the origin."

Mañjuśrī said, "What is the origin of false discrimination?"

Vimalakīrti replied, "Distorted thoughts are the origin."

Mañjuśrī said, "What is the origin of distorted thoughts?"

Vimalakīrti replied, "Nonabiding is the origin."

Mañjuśrī said, "What is the origin of nonabiding?"

Vimalakīrti replied, "Because it is nonabiding, there is no origin. Mañjuśrī! All phenomena are established on the basis of nonabiding."

At that time there was a goddess in Vimalakīrti's room. Seeing those great Bodhisattvas listen to the Dharma being taught, she manifested herself and showered heavenly flowers upon the Bodhisattvas and Śrāvakas. The flowers that rained on the Bodhisattvas all fell to the floor, but those that rained on the Śrāvakas remained, and did not fall to the floor. Even with all of their spiritual powers, the Śrāvakas could not remove them.

7.074 Then the goddess asked Śāriputra, "Why do you want to remove these flowers?"

Śāriputra replied, "These flowers are not in accord with the Dharma, so I am trying to remove them."

The goddess said, "Do not say these flowers are not in accord with the Dharma. Why? These flowers do not discriminate. It is you, Humane One, who gives rise to discrimination. When those who have left the home life to follow the Buddhadharma make discriminations, this is not in accord with the Dharma. The absence of discrimination is in accord with the Dharma. See these Bodhisattvas, to whom the flowers do not attach. This is because they have cut off all discrimination. This is like how, when people are afraid, nonhumans may gain control of them. In the same way, when people are afraid of birth and death, then forms, sounds, scents, flavors, and tangible objects may gain control of them. Those who have transcended fear cannot be controlled by the five desires. Because you have yet to put an end to your habitual afflictions, these flowers stick to you. They will not stick to those who have put an end to their habitual afflictions."

Then Śāriputra said to the goddess, "Goddess, how long have you been in this room?"

The goddess replied, "I have been in this room, elder, as long as you have been liberated." 7.075

Śāriputra said, "You have been here all that time?"

The goddess replied, "Has it not been that long, elder, since you attained liberation?"

Śāriputra was silent and did not respond.

The goddess said, "Why do you, elder, with all your wisdom, remain silent?"

Śāriputra replied, "Liberation transcends language. So I do not know how to respond."

The goddess said, "Words and language are themselves liberation. Why is that? Liberation is not internal, external, or in between. Nor are words internal, external, or in between. Therefore, Śāriputra, do not speak of liberation apart from language. Why not? Everything is liberation."

Śāriputra said, "Is liberation not to free oneself from desire, anger, and delusion?"

The goddess replied, "For those with overweening pride, the Buddha taught that to free oneself from desire, anger, and delusion leads to liberation. For those without overweening pride, the Buddha taught that desire, anger, and delusion are just liberation."

Śāriputra said, "Excellent, excellent, goddess! What have you attained, what have you realized, that you are so eloquent?"

The goddess replied, "Śāriputra, there is nothing 7.076
I have attained or realized. It is because of this that I have such eloquence. Why is that? If there were something I had attained or realized, then I would be disparaging the Buddhadharma through my overweening pride."

Śāriputra asked the goddess, "Of the Three Vehicles, which one do you aspire to?"

The goddess replied, "I teach living beings through the Dharma of Śrāvakas, so I am a Śrāvaka. I teach living beings through dependent arising, so I am a Pratyekhabuddha. I teach living beings through the Dharma of great compassion, so I am a practitioner of the Great Vehicle. Śāriputra! Just as those who enter a forest filled with campaka flowers smell only campaka fragrance and no other fragrance, in the same way, those who enter this room will only delight in the fragrance of the Buddhas' merit, and will not delight in the fragrance of the Śrāvakas' or Pratyekabuddhas' merit. Śāriputra! All the Śakras, brahmās, four heavenly kings, gods, dragons, ghosts, and spirits who have come here to listen to the Proper Dharma taught by this venerable person will delight in the fragrance of the Buddhas' merit and leave this room having resolved upon awakening.

"Śāriputra! I have been in this room for twelve years. Since I first came here, I have never heard the Dharma of Śrāvakas or Pratyekabuddhas; I have only heard about the Bodhisattvas' great kindness and compassion and the Buddhas' inconceivable Dharma. Śāriputra! Eight rare and unprecedented phenomena constantly occur in this room.
7.077 What are the eight?

This room is constantly illuminated by a golden light and is equally bright day and night. It is not lit by the radiance of the sun or moon. This is the first rare and unprecedented phenomenon.

Those who enter this room will not be afflicted by any defilements. This is the second rare and unprecedented phenomenon.

Śakras, brahmās, four heavenly kings, and Bodhisattvas from other lands continuously gather in this room. This is the third rare and unprecedented phenomenon.

The six pāramitās and the Dharma of irreversibility are constantly expounded in this room. This is the fourth rare and unprecedented phenomenon.

Heavenly instruments constantly play supreme music in this room, and their strings resound with countless Dharmas as teachings. This is the fifth rare and unprecedented phenomenon.

This room has four great treasuries brimming with a variety of treasures that endlessly fulfill all the wishes of the impoverished and destitute. This is the sixth rare and unprecedented phenomenon.

Śākyamuni Buddha, Amitābha Buddha, Akṣobhya 7.078
Buddha, Jewel Virtue Buddha, Precious Blaze Buddha, Jewel Moon Buddha, Jewel Adornment Buddha, Invincible Buddha, Lion's Roar Buddha, Realizing All Benefits Buddha, and countless Buddhas such as these from all ten directions come to this room at the mere thought of this venerable person. They extensively teach all Buddhas' treasury of esoteric and essential Dharma and depart after teaching. This is the seventh rare and unprecedented phenomenon.

All the magnificently embellished heavenly palaces and Buddhas' pure lands appear in this room. This is the eighth rare and unprecedented phenomenon.

"Śāriputra! These eight rare and unprecedented phenomena constantly occur in this room. Who, having witnessed such inconceivable things, would delight in the Dharma of Srāvakas?"

Śāriputra said, "Why have you not transformed your female body?"

The goddess replied, "For twelve years, I have sought the female state of being, but in vain. What is there to transform? Suppose a magician conjured a woman, and someone were to ask her, 'Why don't you transform your female body?' Would that person be asking a proper question?"

Śāriputra replied, "No. An illusion does not have any fixed form. How could it transform?"

7.079 The goddess said, "Likewise, all phenomena are like an illusion without any fixed form. So how can you ask me, 'Why have you not transformed your female body?'"

Then the goddess used her spiritual powers to transform Śāriputra's appearance into her own, while she assumed the appearance of Śāriputra. Then she asked him, "Why don't you transform your female body?"

Śāriputra, who now looked like the goddess, replied, "How have I been transformed into this female form?"

The goddess replied, "Śāriputra, if you can transform this female body, then all women should be able to transform theirs. Just as you, Śāriputra, who are not a woman, now appear in a female body, so it is for all women, who appear to have female bodies but are not women. Therefore, the Buddha said, 'Phenomena are neither male nor female.'"

The goddess then withdrew her spiritual powers, whereupon Śāriputra resumed his original form. Then she asked Śāriputra, "Where is that female form of yours now?"

Śāriputra replied, "The female form does not exist yet does not not exist."

The goddess said, "All phenomena are just like this. They do not exist yet do not not exist. That which does not exist yet does not not exist was taught by the Buddha."

Śāriputra asked the goddess, "When your present state of being comes to an end, in what way will you be reborn?"

The goddess replied, "I will be reborn in the same way as a Buddha."

Śāriputra said, "A Buddha does not come to an end, nor does he come into being."

The goddess replied, "Likewise, living beings do not come to an end, nor do they come into being."

Śāriputra asked the goddess, "How long will it take 7.080
for you to attain anuttarā samyaksaṃbodhi?"

The goddess replied, "When you, Śāriputra, return to the state of an ordinary being, then I will attain anuttarā samyaksaṃbodhi."

Śāriputra said, "It is not possible for me to return to the state of an ordinary being."

The goddess replied, "Then it is not possible for me to attain anuttarā samyaksaṃbodhi. Why not? Bodhi abides nowhere; therefore, it cannot be attained."

Śāriputra said, "Then what would you say about those Buddhas, as many as the grains of sand in the Ganges, who are attaining, have attained, and will attain anuttarā samyaksaṃbodhi?"

The goddess replied, "It is only through mundane words and numbers that we speak of the three periods of time. This does not mean that bodhi itself has past, present, or future." The goddess then asked, "Śāriputra, have you attained Arhatship?"

Śāriputra replied, "Having realized that there is nothing to attain, I attained it."

The goddess said, "In the same way, the attainment of Buddhas and Bodhisattvas comes as a result of their realizing that there is nothing to attain."

Then Vimalakīrti addressed Śāriputra, saying, "This goddess has made offerings to ninety-two koṭis of Buddhas. She has effortless mastery of all Bodhisattvas' spiritual powers, and all her vows have been fulfilled. Having attained the patient acceptance of the nonarising of phenomena, she abides in irreversibility. By virtue of her past vows, she can appear at will and teach living beings."

THE PATH TO BUDDHAHOOD

CHAPTER 8

At that time Mañjuśrī asked Vimalakīrti, "How does a Bodhisattva walk the path to Buddhahood?"

Vimalakīrti replied, "A Bodhisattva walks the path to Buddhahood by walking what is not the path."

Mañjuśrī said, "How does a Bodhisattva walk what is not the path?"

Vimalakīrti replied,

"When Bodhisattvas are in the five relentless
hells, they are free of affliction and anger.
When they are in the hells, they are free of
offenses and defilements.
When they are in the animal realm, they are free
of the faults of ignorance and arrogance.
When they are in the realm of hungry ghosts,
they are replete with merit.
When they are in the realms of form and
the formless, they do not regard them as
superior.

8.081 They appear to have desire yet remain apart from attachment.
They appear to have anger yet harbor no anger toward living beings.
They appear to be ignorant yet discipline their minds by means of wisdom.
They appear to be stingy yet renounce everything internal and external, not even sparing their body or life.
They appear to violate the precepts yet are firmly established in the pure precepts and are afraid to commit even the smallest offense.
They appear to act out of anger yet are always patient and kind.
They appear to act lazy yet diligently cultivate merit and virtue.
They appear to be distracted yet are always in samādhi.
They appear to be ignorant yet completely master worldly and world-transcending wisdom.

They appear to resort to flattery and deceit yet excel at skillful means while according with the principles of the sūtras.
They appear to be arrogant yet act as a bridge for living beings.
They appear to be afflicted, yet their minds remain forever pure.
They appear to follow demonic ways yet accord with the Buddhas' wisdom and no other teachings.
They appear as Śrāvakas yet teach living beings the unprecedented Dharma.
8.082 They appear as Pratyekabuddhas yet perfect great compassion in order to teach living beings.

They appear to be poor yet have jeweled hands of inexhaustible merit.
They appear to be deformed and crippled yet are replete with the adornment of all magnificent hallmarks.
They appear to be lowly yet are in the Buddhas' family and are replete with all merit.
They appear to be feeble and ugly yet attain a Nārāyaṇa body that all living beings delight to see.
They appear to undergo old age and sickness yet have forever severed the root of sickness and transcended the fear of death.

They appear to possess all the necessities of life 8.083
yet desire nothing and constantly contemplate impermanence.
They appear to have wives, concubines, and ladies-in-waiting yet have forever left behind the muck of the five desires.
They appear to be inarticulate and dull-witted yet command great eloquence and have a perfect memory that forgets nothing.
They appear to employ improper means yet rescue living beings with proper means.
They appear to walk many paths yet remain detached from the causes and conditions therein.
They appear to enter nirvāṇa yet do not put an end to birth and death.

"Mañjuśrī, if Bodhisattvas walk what is not the path in this way, they walk the path to Buddhahood."

Vimalakīrti then asked Mañjuśrī Bodhisattva, "What is the seed of the Tathāgata?"

Mañjuśrī replied,

8.084 "The existence of a body is the seed.
Ignorance and craving are the seed.
Greed, anger, and delusion are the seed.
The four distorted views are the seed.
The five hindrances are the seed.
The six sense faculties are the seed.
The seven abodes of consciousness[32] are the seed.
The eight improper practices are the seed.
The nine states of affliction[33] are the seed.
And the ten unwholesome deeds are the seed.

"In short, the sixty-two [wrong] views and all afflictions are the seed of Buddhahood."

Vimalakīrti said, "What does that mean?"

Mañjuśrī replied, "Those who seek awakening through the realization of the unconditioned cannot aspire to anuttarā samyaksaṃbodhi. Just as lotus flowers do not grow on high plateaus but rather in the lowly mud of wetlands, those who seek awakening through the realization of the unconditioned cannot aspire to the Buddhas' Dharma. Rather, it is only amid the mire of afflictions that living beings bring forth the aspiration for the Buddhas' Dharma.

8.085 "Furthermore, seeds planted in empty space will never grow; only in soil fertilized with dung and manure can they flourish. Those who seek awakening through the realization of the unconditioned cannot take root in the Buddhas' Dharma. On the other hand, those with a view of self as large as Mount Sumeru are still able to bring forth the resolve for anuttarā samyaksaṃbodhi and take root in the Buddhas' Dharma. Therefore, you should know that all afflictions are the seed of the Tathāgata. Just as priceless pearls cannot be obtained without diving into the ocean, the treasure of omniscient wisdom cannot be attained without entering the sea of afflictions."

Then Mahākāśyapa said in praise, "Good indeed, good indeed, Mañjuśrī! Well said! Just as you say, afflictions are the field in which to plant the seed of the Tathāgata. We [Śrāvakas] are not able to bring forth the resolve for anuttarā samyaksaṃbodhi. While even those who commit the five relentless offenses can still aspire to the Buddhas' Dharma, we [Śrāvakas] no longer aspire to it. Just as people whose sense faculties are impaired can no longer enjoy the five desires, we Śrāvakas who have cut off all afflictions can no longer benefit from the Buddhas' Dharma, and no longer aspire to it. Therefore, Mañjuśrī, while ordinary beings are still able to practice in response to the Buddhas' Dharma, Śrāvakas are not. Why is that? When ordinary beings hear the Buddhas' Dharma, they are able to bring forth the unsurpassed resolve for bodhi and ensure the perpetuation of the Three Jewels. Even if we Śrāvakas spent our entire lives listening to the Buddhas' Dharma, the [ten] powers, the [four kinds of] fearlessness, and so on, we still would not bring forth the unsurpassed resolve for bodhi."

Then, in the midst of the assembly, a Bodhisattva 8.086
named Everywhere Manifesting Physical Forms asked Vimalakīrti, "Layman, who are your parents, your wife and children, your relatives, assistants, and acquaintances? Where are your servants, attendants, elephants, horses, and carriages?"

Then Vimalakīrti replied in verse:

The perfection of wisdom is the mother of
Bodhisattvas,
And the perfection of skillful means, their father.
All guiding masters of living beings,
Without exception, are born from these.

Dharma joy is their spouse;
Kindness and compassion are their daughters;
Wholesomeness and honesty are their sons;
And ultimate stillness is their home.

Afflictions are their disciples,
Transformed however the Bodhisattvas wish.
The [thirty-seven] factors of awakening are their spiritual teachers,
Through which they attain true awakening.

8.087 The pāramitās and myriad practices are their companions,
And the four methods of attraction, their ladies-in-waiting.
Songs, ballads, and verses that resound with the Dharma:
Bodhisattvas regard these as their music.

In their garden of dhāraṇīs
Are trees of nonoutflow Dharma,
Pure, wondrous flowers of awakening,
And the fruit of wisdom and liberation.

The pool of the eight liberations,
Brimming with the water of samādhi
And covered with the seven pure flowers,
Washes clean those who are undefiled.

The five spiritual powers are their elephants and horses;
The Great Vehicle is their carriage.
With single-mindedness as their driver,
They travel along the eightfold path.

Perfect hallmarks adorn their countenance.
Myriad excellent qualities ennoble their
appearance.
Conscience and remorse are their superb
garments,
And their profound mind is a flower garland.

They are rich with the seven treasures.
Through teaching, their treasures grow.
They embody what they teach,
Making dedications to bring about great benefit.

Their bed is the four dhyānas,
Which arise from a pure life.
Extensive learning increases their wisdom,
Which they hear as the sound of self-awakening.

The sweet dew of Dharma is their food, 8.088
The flavor of liberation, their beverage.
Purifying the mind is their bath,
And the precepts are their ointment.

With courage and strength unsurpassed,
They vanquish the thieves of affliction.
Having subdued the four demons and raised the
banner of victory,
They establish a place for awakening.

Despite knowing that there is no arising or
ceasing,
They take rebirth in order to guide beings,
Appearing in every land
Like the sun, which all can see.

They make offerings in the ten directions
To countless koṭis of Tathāgatas.

Between the Buddhas and themselves,
They make no distinction.

Even though they know that Buddhalands
And living beings are all empty,
They always create pure lands
And teach all living beings.

Fearless Bodhisattvas,
In an instant, are able to manifest
Various kinds of living beings,
With their forms, sounds, and mannerisms.

Fully aware of all the activities of demons,
Bodhisattvas appear to follow their conduct;
Through the skillful means of wisdom,
They can appear in whatever way they wish.

8.089 They appear to age, fall ill, and die
So that all living beings are led to maturity.
Realizing that all of this is illusory, Bodhisattvas
Break through and free themselves of all
hindrance.

They manifest the inferno at the end of an eon,
Which incinerates the heavens and the earth,
So that ordinary people, who believe in
permanence,
Are awakened to impermanence.

Numberless koṭis of living beings
All come to implore the Bodhisattvas
To visit their homes all at once
And inspire them to strive toward Buddhahood.

Worldly writings, spells and sorcery,
Talents, skills, and all kinds of artistry:

Bodhisattvas appear to engage with all
these things
In order to benefit all living beings.

In order to dispel the delusions of others,
They leave the home life
And join all the religious orders of the world,
Yet they never fall into wrong views.

They may appear as sun gods or moon gods,
As brahmās or heavenly kings;
At times they may appear
As earth, water, wind, or even fire.

When an epidemic occurs in the midst of 8.090
calamities,
They appear as medicinal herbs.
Anyone who takes these herbs
Will have their sickness cured and all poison
eradicated.

When a famine occurs in the midst of calamities,
They appear as food and drink.
After satisfying the hungry and thirsty,
They teach them the Dharma.

When a war occurs in the midst of calamities,
Bodhisattvas bring forth great sympathy.
They transform living beings,
Settling them on the ground of noncontention.

If there is a great battle,
Bodhisattvas cause each side to be equal in
strength.
Manifesting their mighty power,
They bring about harmony and peace.

Throughout all lands,
Wherever there are hells,
They constantly enter them
To rescue beings from suffering and anguish.

Throughout all lands,
Animals devour one another.
Bodhisattvas are born among them
In order to benefit them.

They may appear to enjoy the five desires
While also practicing dhyāna,
Utterly confusing the demons
So they cannot get the better of them.

8.091 For a lotus to grow amid fire and flames
Is said to be very rare.
To practice dhyāna amid desire
Is just as unusual.

They may appear as courtesans
To seduce those who are lustful,
Enticing them with desire at first,
But eventually leading them to Buddhahood.

They may appear as the mayor of a city,
A leader among merchants,
A national master[34] or an official,
In order to benefit living beings.

For those who live in poverty,
They make inexhaustible treasuries appear
As a means to exhort and guide them
To make the resolve for bodhi.

To those with pride and conceit,
They appear as a person of great power

In order to dispel their arrogance
And establish them in the unsurpassed path.

They stand before the terrified multitudes
And bring them comfort,
First lending them fearlessness
And then inspiring them to resolve upon bodhi.

They may appear as a ṛṣi[35] with the five spiritual
powers
Who has left all sexual desire behind.
Guiding all living beings, Bodhisattvas lead them
To abide in precepts, patience, and kindness.

Seeing those in need of service, 8.092
They appear as their servants,
Delighting them by fulfilling their every wish
And inspiring them to resolve upon bodhi.

Fulfilling whatever others require
To embark upon the Buddhas' Path,
Bodhisattvas, through skillful means,
Satisfy every need without exception.

Having countless ways such as these,
That which they practice is limitless.
Their wisdom knows no bounds
And rescues numberless living beings.

Even if all Buddhas,
For countless koṭis of eons,
Praised their merit and virtue,
They would still be unable to finish.

Hearing this Dharma,
Who would not resolve upon bodhi—
Who except the worthless,
The ignorant, and the unwise?

ENTERING THE DHARMA-DOOR OF NONDUALITY

CHAPTER 9

At that time Vimalakīrti said to the assembly of Bodhisattvas, "Humane Ones, how does the Bodhisattva enter the Dharma-door of nonduality? Each of you should speak as you wish."

A Bodhisattva in the assembly named Self-Mastery in the Dharma said, "Humane Ones, coming into being and ceasing to be are a duality. Phenomena have never come into being, so they cannot now cease to be. To attain the patient acceptance of the nonarising of phenomena by means of this understanding is to enter the Dharma-door of nonduality."

Bodhisattva Guardian of Virtue said, "Self and what pertains to a self are a duality. When there is a self, there is what pertains to a self. To realize that when there is no self, there is nothing that pertains to a self is to enter the Dharma-door of nonduality."

Bodhisattva Steady Gaze said, "Sense perception 9.093
and the absence of sense perception are a duality. When

phenomena are not perceived, there is nothing to attain. Because there is nothing to attain, there is nothing to grasp, nothing to renounce, nothing to create, and nothing to act upon. To realize this is to enter the Dharma-door of nonduality."

Bodhisattva Crown of Virtue said, "Defilement and purity are a duality. In seeing the true nature of defilement, one does away with the notion of purity and thereby accords with ultimate stillness. This is to enter the Dharma-door of nonduality."

Bodhisattva Sublime Constellation said, "Distraction and concentration are a duality. Without distraction, there is no concentration; without concentration, there is no discrimination. To thoroughly understand this is to enter the Dharma-door of nonduality."

Bodhisattva Kind Eyes said, "Characteristics and the absence of characteristics are a duality. To understand that characteristics are the absence of characteristics without clinging to the absence of characteristics is to realize impartiality. To realize this is to enter the Dharma-door of nonduality."

Bodhisattva Wondrous Arms said, "The mind of a Bodhisattva and the mind of a Śrāvaka are a duality. To see the mind as intrinsically empty and illusory, in that neither the mind of a Bodhisattva nor the mind of a Śrāvaka exists, is to enter the Dharma-door of nonduality."

9.094 Bodhisattva Puṣya[36] said, "Wholesome and unwholesome are a duality. Not to give rise to wholesome and unwholesome, and thereby to fully realize the state in which all characteristics are absent, is to enter the Dharma-door of nonduality."

Bodhisattva Lion said, "Transgression and nontransgression are a duality. To thoroughly understand the nature of transgression is to realize that it is no different from nontransgression. To discern this with vajra wisdom and realize that there are neither bonds nor liberation is to enter the Dharma-door of nonduality."

Bodhisattva Lion's Will said, "Outflow and nonoutflow are a duality. To realize the equality of all phenomena is to put an end to the discrimination between outflow and nonoutflow. Not to attach to their existence or cling to their nonexistence is to enter the Dharma-door of nonduality."

Bodhisattva Pure Understanding said, "The conditioned and the unconditioned are a duality. To free one's mind from calculation is to make it like empty space. To employ pure wisdom without obstruction is to enter the Dharma-door of nonduality."

Bodhisattva Nārāyaṇa said, "The worldly and the transcendent are a duality. To see the mundane world as empty is to transcend the world. Neither entering the world nor transcending it, with one's involvement in the world neither increasing nor fading away: this is to enter the Dharma-door of nonduality."

Bodhisattva Good Intention said, "Birth and death 9.095
and nirvāṇa are a duality. To see the nature of birth and death is to free oneself from birth and death, which are free from bondage and liberation and not subject to coming into being or ceasing to be. To realize this is to enter the Dharma-door of nonduality."

Bodhisattva Manifestation of Insight said, "The finite and the infinite are a duality. If everything is fundamentally ultimate, then both the finite and the infinite are infinite. Yet the infinite is no different from emptiness. In emptiness, neither finite nor infinite exists. To realize this is to enter the Dharma-door of nonduality."

Bodhisattva Universal Guardian said, "Self and nonself are a duality. If even the self cannot be attained, how could nonself be attained? To see the true nature of the self and no longer discriminate between self and nonself is to enter the Dharma-door of nonduality."

Bodhisattva Heavenly Lightning said, "Understanding and ignorance are a duality. The true nature of ignorance is understanding, yet even that understanding cannot be grasped. To put an end to all reckoning and regard these two as equal and nondual is to enter the Dharma-door of nonduality."

Bodhisattva Delightful to See said, "Form and the absence of form are a duality. Form itself is the absence of form. The absence of form does not come about at the extinction of form. Form is inherently nonexistent. It is the same for sense perception, cognition, and mental formations. Consciousness and the absence of consciousness are a duality. Consciousness itself is the absence of consciousness. The absence of consciousness does not come about at the extinction of consciousness. Consciousness is inherently nonexistent. To fully comprehend this principle is to enter the Dharma-door of nonduality."

9.096 Bodhisattva Shining of Light said, "The four elements and the element of emptiness are a duality. The nature of the four elements is identical with the nature of the element of emptiness. As their existence in the past and future is empty, their existence in the present is also empty. To understand the nature of the elements in this way is to enter the Dharma-door of nonduality."

Bodhisattva Wondrous Resolve said, "The eye and forms are a duality. To understand the nature of the eye and thereby free oneself from greed, anger, and delusion with respect to forms is to realize ultimate stillness. In the same way, the ear and sounds, the nose and scents, the tongue and flavors, the body and tangible objects, and the mind and mental objects are dualities. To understand the nature of the mind and thereby free oneself from greed, anger, and delusion with respect to mental objects is to realize ultimate stillness. To establish oneself in this is to enter the Dharma-door of nonduality."

Bodhisattva Infinite Resolve said, "Giving and the dedication of merit [from giving] to the attainment of omniscient wisdom are a duality. The nature of giving is just the nature of the dedication of merit to the attainment of omniscient wisdom. In the same way, the upholding of precepts, patience, vigor, dhyāna, and wisdom and the dedication of merit [from them] to the attainment of omniscient wisdom are dualities. The nature of wisdom is the nature of the dedication of merit [from wisdom] to the attainment of omniscient wisdom. To realize that these are one and the same is to enter the Dharma-door of nonduality."

Bodhisattva Profound Wisdom said, "Emptiness, marklessness, and effortlessness are dualities. What is empty is also markless; what is markless is also effortless. That which is empty, markless, and effortless brings about the cessation of thought. In entering one door of liberation, one enters all three doors of liberation. This is to enter the Dharma-door of nonduality."

Bodhisattva Serene Faculties said, "The Buddha, the 9.097
Dharma, and the Sangha are dualities. The Buddha is the Dharma; the Dharma is the Sangha. Like empty space, the Three Jewels are unconditioned. So too are all phenomena. To practice in accord with this is to enter the Dharma-door of nonduality."

Bodhisattva Unobstructed Mind said, "The body and the cessation of the body are a duality. The body itself is the cessation of the body. Why is that? To see the body as it really is, is to end the discrimination between the body and the cessation of the body. The body and the cessation of the body are nondual and without difference. Not to be frightened or disturbed by this is to enter the Dharma-door of nonduality."

Bodhisattva Supreme Goodness said, "Wholesome actions of body, speech, and mind are dualities. These three are free of the characteristic of action. The nonaction of the body is the nonaction of speech; the nonaction of speech is the nonaction of the mind. The nonaction of these three is the nonaction of all phenomena. To thus accord with the wisdom of nonaction is to enter the Dharma-door of nonduality."

Bodhisattva Field of Blessings said, "Meritorious deeds, unwholesome deeds, and neutral deeds are dualities.[37] The true nature of these three is empty. In emptiness, there are no meritorious deeds, no unwholesome deeds, and no neutral deeds. Not to give rise to these three is to enter the Dharma-door of nonduality."

9.098 Bodhisattva Flower Garland said, "That the self gives rise to the other is a duality. To see the self as it really is, is not to give rise to duality. Not abiding in such a duality puts an end to the discrimination between self and other. To put an end to such discrimination is to enter the Dharma-door of nonduality."

Bodhisattva Treasury of Virtue said, "That there is something to attain is a duality. When there is nothing to attain, there is no grasping or renouncing. To be without grasping and renouncing is to enter the Dharma-door of nonduality."

Bodhisattva Superior Moon said, "Darkness and light are a duality. Without darkness and light, there is no duality. Why is that? In the samādhi of the cessation of sense perception and cognition, there is neither darkness nor light. It is the same for everything. To realize the inherent equality of all things is to enter the Dharma-door of nonduality."

Bodhisattva Jewelled Mudrā said, "To delight in nirvāṇa and loathe the mundane world are a duality. To neither delight in nirvāṇa nor loathe the mundane world is to be without duality. Why is that? If there is bondage, there is liberation. If there is no bondage, why seek liberation? Freedom from bondage and liberation is freedom from delight and loathing. To realize this is to enter the Dharma-door of nonduality."

Bodhisattva King Crowned with Pearls said, "The proper path and the improper path are a duality. To abide on the proper path is not to discriminate between proper and improper. To transcend their duality is to enter the Dharma-door of nonduality."

Bodhisattva Delighting in Truth said, "The true and the false are a duality. To see is not to see the true, let alone the false. Why is that? The wisdom eye can see what the physical eye cannot. The wisdom eye does not see, yet does not fail to see everything. To realize this is to enter the Dharma-door of nonduality."

After each and every Bodhisattva had spoken, they asked Mañjuśrī, "How does the Bodhisattva enter the Dharma-door of nonduality?"

Mañjuśrī said, "As I see it, not to offer words, explanations, comments, or opinions regarding anything and to remain apart from questions and answers is to enter the Dharma-door of nonduality."

Then Mañjuśrī asked Vimalakīrti, "Now that we have all expressed our understanding, what would you, Humane One, say about how a Bodhisattva should enter the Dharma-door of nonduality?"

At that time Vimalakīrti remained silent and did 9.099
not say a word.

Mañjuśrī exclaimed in praise, "Good indeed, good indeed! To be free even of words and language is truly to enter the Dharma-door of nonduality."

When this chapter on entering the Dharma-door of nonduality was taught, five thousand Bodhisattvas in the assembly entered the Dharma-door of nonduality and realized—the patient acceptance of the nonarising of phenomena.

BUDDHA COLLECTION OF SUPREME FRAGRANCES

CHAPTER 10

Thereupon, Śāriputra thought, "It will soon be noon. What will all these Bodhisattvas eat?"

Vimalakīrti, knowing Śāriputra's thoughts, said to him, "Humane One, you have already accepted and put into practice the eight kinds of liberation taught by the Buddha. How can you think about food while listening to the Dharma? If you want to eat, then wait a moment! I will let you taste something you've never had before."

Vimalakīrti then immediately entered samādhi. By means of his spiritual powers, he showed the great assembly a Buddhaland called Myriad Fragrances located in the worlds above, beyond as many Buddhalands as the grains of sand in forty-two Ganges Rivers. The Buddha there was named Collection of Supreme Fragrances. Compared with the fragrances of humans and gods in the Buddhalands of the ten directions, those of that land were foremost. That land had no Śrāvakas or Pratyekabuddhas, only a multitude of pure, great

Bodhisattvas to whom the Buddha expounded the Dharma. In that land, all the pavilions were made of fragrance; the paths and gardens were fragrant; and the fragrance of the food there permeated countless worlds throughout the ten directions. Just as that Buddha was sitting down to eat together with all those Bodhisattvas, a multitude of gods all named Fragrant Garland brought forth the resolve for anuttarā samyaksaṃbodhi. Everyone in the assembly saw them make offerings to that Buddha and the Bodhisattvas.

10.100 Then Vimalakīrti asked the assembled Bodhisattvas, "Humane Ones, who among you can go to that Buddha for food?" But all of them were silenced by Mañjuśrī's awe-inspiring spiritual power. Vimalakīrti said, "Humane Ones, is none of you ashamed?"

Mañjuśrī said, "Didn't the Buddha say not to look down on those not yet learned?"

Thereupon, without rising from his seat before the assembly, Vimalakīrti manifested a transformation Bodhisattva whose hallmarks were radiant with light. Endowed with supreme, awe-inspiring virtue, these hallmarks eclipsed the assembly.

Vimalakīrti then said to this Bodhisattva, "Go up to the worlds above. Beyond Buddhalands as many as the grains of sand in forty-two Ganges Rivers, there is a Buddhaland called Myriad Fragrances. The Buddha there, named Collection of Supreme Fragrances, is at this moment sitting and eating together with all the Bodhisattvas. Go there and convey my words as follows: 'Vimalakīrti bows with his head at the World Honored One's feet and, with boundless respect, inquires after his well-being: Are you free from sickness and worry? Are you healthy and at ease? For the sake of doing the Buddha's work in the Sahā world, I wish to have what remains of the World Honored One's meal, in order to enable those who delight in the lesser Dharma to propagate the great Path, and so that the Tathāgata's reputation will extend everywhere.'"

At that time, in the presence of the assembly, the transformation Bodhisattva immediately ascended to the worlds above; and the entire assembly saw him depart. After he arrived at the Buddhaland Myriad Fragrances and bowed at the Buddha's feet, they heard him say, "Vimalakīrti bows his head at the World Honored One's feet and, with boundless respect, inquires after his well-being: Are you free from sickness and worry? Are you healthy and at ease? For the sake of doing the Buddha's work in the Sahā world, I wish to have what remains of the World Honored One's meal, in order to enable those who delight in the lesser Dharma to propagate the great Path, and so that the Tathāgata's reputation will extend everywhere." 10.101

When the Great Beings there saw the transformation Bodhisattva, they exclaimed at such an unprecedented sight: "Where has this venerable person come from just now? Where is the Sahā world? What is meant by 'those who delight in the lesser Dharma'?"

They asked the Buddha these questions, and the Buddha said to them, "In the lower direction, beyond as many Buddhalands as the grains of sand in forty-two Ganges Rivers, there is a world called Sahā. The Buddha there is named Śakyamuni. In the troubled age of the five turbidities, he sets forth the teaching of the Path for the sake of those who delight in the lesser Dharma. There is a Bodhisattva there named Vimalakīrti, who abides in the inconceivable liberation and explains the Dharma for all the Bodhisattvas. He has sent this transformation body here to honor my name and praise this land, enabling those Bodhisattvas to increase in merit and virtue."

The Bodhisattvas wondered, "What has that person done that he can manifest this kind of transformation body 10.102

and his virtue, fearlessness, and ability to travel anywhere at will are such as this?"

The Buddha replied, "His accomplishments are exceedingly great! He sends transformation bodies throughout the ten directions to carry out the Buddhas' work and benefit living beings."

Tathāgata Collection of Supreme Fragrances thereupon took a bowl perfumed with myriad fragrances, filled it with fragrant food, and gave it to the transformation Bodhisattva. Then the nine million Bodhisattvas there spoke in unison, saying, "We wish to go to the Sahā world to make offerings to Śakyamuni Buddha and to see Vimalakīrti and the rest of the multitude of Bodhisattvas."

The Buddha said, "You may go. However, in order to avoid confusing the living beings there, and to prevent them from giving rise to attachment, you should restrain your bodies from exuding fragrance. You should also renounce your original forms to avoid making those who aspire to be Bodhisattvas feel ashamed of their inferiority. Furthermore, you must not harbor thoughts of contempt or belittlement toward them, or regard them as having hindrances. Why is that? The lands of the ten directions are like empty space.[38] Furthermore, in order to teach and transform those who delight in the lesser Dharma, the Buddhas do not always reveal their pure lands in their entirety."

Having accepted the bowl of food, the transformation Bodhisattva, accompanied by the nine million Bodhisattvas and aided by the Buddha's awe-inspiring dignity and Vimalakīrti's power, suddenly vanished from that world and, in an instant, arrived at Vimalakīrti's house.

10.103 Vimalakīrti then manifested nine million lion thrones, as finely adorned as the previous thrones, upon which those Bodhisattvas seated themselves. The transformation Bodhisattva gave the bowl filled with fragrant food to Vimalakīrti, and the aroma of the food perfumed the city of Vaiśālī as well as the entire trichiliocosm. When the brāhmaṇas and laypeople all smelled this fragrant aroma, they felt exhilarated in body and mind and praised such an unprecedented experience. The leading elder [of Vaiśālī], Moon Canopy, accompanied by eighty-four thousand people, went to Vimalakīrti's house. All of them were greatly delighted to see the many Bodhisattvas and their lofty, broad, and finely adorned lion thrones. Having bowed to the Bodhisattvas and Śrāvakas, they withdrew to one side. Various gods of the earth, gods of space, and gods of the realms of desire and form, upon smelling the fragrance, also went to Vimalakīrti's house.

Then Vimalakīrti told Śāriputra and all the other 10.104
Śrāvakas, "Humane Ones, you may come and eat this meal, which is as delicious as the Tathāgatas' sweet dew and is infused with great compassion. Do not eat it with a narrow mind, for you will not be able to digest it."

But some Śrāvakas thought differently: "There isn't much food. How could it feed everyone in such a great assembly?"

The transformation Bodhisattva said, "Do not use the scanty virtue and wisdom of a Śrāvaka to measure the Tathāgatas' measureless merit and wisdom! The four oceans might run dry, but this food cannot be exhausted. Even if everyone in the assembly ate portions the size of Mount Sumeru [at every meal] over the course of an eon, this food would not run out. Why not? The leftovers of those who have perfected the merit of inexhaustible precepts, samādhi, wisdom, liberation, and the knowledge of liberation are utterly inexhaustible." Then the transformation Bodhisattva fed the entire assembly with that single bowl of food, but the food did not run out. All the Bodhisattvas, Śrāvakas, gods, and humans who ate it felt calm and happy, just like the

Bodhisattvas in the Land Adorned with All Joys. From their pores came a fragrance like that of the trees in the land Myriad Fragrances.

10.105 At that time Vimalakīrti asked the Bodhisattvas from the land Myriad Fragrances, "By what means does Tathāgata Collection of Supreme Fragrances teach the Dharma?"

Those Bodhisattvas replied, "The Tathāgata of our land does not use words. Instead, he uses myriad fragrances to lead all gods and humans to undertake the practice of the precepts. Each and every Bodhisattva sits beneath the fragrant trees. Upon smelling the wonderful fragrance of these trees, they attain the samādhi of the treasury of all virtue. All those who attain this samādhi completely perfect the Bodhisattvas' merit and virtue."

All of the Bodhisattvas then asked Vimalakīrti, "By what means does World Honored One Śakyamuni teach the Dharma?"

Vimalakīrti replied, "The living beings of this land are obstinate and hard to teach. Therefore, the Buddha uses stern words to teach living beings, telling them,

> 'Such is the hell realm.
> Such is the animal realm.
> Such is the realm of hungry ghosts.
> Such is the place of difficult circumstances.[39]
> Such is the place where foolish people are born.
> Such is misconduct of the body, and such are its consequences.
> Such is misconduct of speech, and such are its consequences.
> Such is misconduct of the mind, and such are its consequences.

Such is killing, and such are its consequences.
Such is stealing, and such are its consequences.
Such is sexual misconduct, and such are its consequences.
Such is false speech, and such are its consequences.
Such is divisive speech, and such are its consequences.
Such is harsh speech, and such are its consequences.
Such is idle chatter, and such are its consequences.

Such are greed and envy, and such are their consequences. 10.106
Such are anger and affliction, and such are their consequences.
Such are wrong views, and such are their consequences.
Such is stinginess, and such are its consequences.
Such is transgression of the precepts, and such are its consequences.
Such is hatred, and such are its consequences.
Such is indolence, and such are its consequences.
Such is scatteredness, and such are its consequences.
Such is ignorance, and such are its consequences.

Such is taking the precepts, such is upholding the precepts, and such is violation of the precepts.
Such is what should be done, and such is what should not be done.
Such is obstruction, and such is the absence of obstruction.

10.107 Such is the commission of offenses, and such is the absolution of offenses.
Such is purity, and such is defilement.
Such are outflows, and such is the freedom from outflows.
Such are improper ways, and such is the proper Path.
Such is the conditioned, and such is the unconditioned.
Such is the worldly, and such is nirvāṇa.'

"Because those who are difficult to teach are monkey-minded, only by various means can the Buddha regulate and tame their minds. For example, elephants and horses may be obstinate and unyielding; therefore, one trains them by inflicting upon them many severe pains, even to the point of piercing their bones. Only then are they subdued. In the same way, for living beings who are stubborn and difficult to teach, the Buddha uses harsh and severe words to lead them to observe the vinaya."

Hearing this, all of the Bodhisattvas exclaimed, "How unprecedented! Just as the World Honored One Śakyamuni Buddha conceals his boundless powers of self-mastery in order to liberate living beings by means of Dharma that is suitable to the wretched, all of the Bodhisattvas also endure hardship, show humility, and are reborn in this Buddhaland through their boundless great compassion."

10.108 Vimalakīrti replied, "Indeed! It is as you say. The great compassion that the Bodhisattvas of this land have toward living beings is unshakable. Thus, what they obtain in a single life through benefiting the living beings of this world exceeds what one can obtain by cultivating in other lands for hundreds of thousands of eons. Why? This Sahā world has ten wholesome practices that do not exist in any other pure land.

"What are these ten?

Gathering in the poor by means of giving.
Gathering in those who transgress by means of the precepts.
Gathering in the angry by means of patience.
Gathering in the indolent by means of vigor.
Gathering in the unfocused by means of samādhi.
Gathering in the ignorant by means of wisdom.
Liberating those in the eight difficult conditions by means of teaching the Dharma of eradicating difficult conditions.
Taking across those who are content with the Lesser Vehicle by means of the Great Vehicle Dharma.
Helping those who lack virtue by means of good roots.
And bringing living beings to maturity by means of the four methods of attraction."

Then the Bodhisattvas asked, "How many practices must Bodhisattvas perfect in order to make their conduct in this world flawless, so that they can be born in a pure land?" 10.109

Vimalakīrti replied, "Bodhisattvas must perfect eight practices in order to make their conduct in this world flawless, so that they can be born in a pure land. What are these eight?

They benefit living beings without expecting anything in return.
They endure all kinds of suffering and distress on behalf of all living beings while giving away all of their merit without reservation.
They regard all living beings equally while humbling themselves without difficulty.

They regard all Bodhisattvas as Buddhas.
They do not give rise to doubt when hearing sūtras they have never heard before.
They do not oppose Śrāvakas.
Because they are not jealous of the offerings made to others or arrogant about the offerings they themselves receive, they are thereby able to subdue their minds.
While constantly reflecting upon their own faults, they never criticize the shortcomings of others, but instead wholeheartedly strive for all merit and virtue.

"These are their eight practices."

When Vimalakīrti and Mañjuśrī taught this Dharma to those in the great assembly, hundreds of thousands of gods and humans resolved upon anuttarā samyaksaṃbodhi and ten thousand Bodhisattvas attained the patient acceptance of the nonarising of phenomena.

BODHISATTVA PRACTICE

CHAPTER 11

At that time the Buddha was teaching the Dharma in the garden of Āmrapālī. Suddenly the land became vast and resplendent, and the entire assembly became golden in color. Ānanda said to the Buddha, "World Honored One! What brings about such an auspicious occurrence? The garden has suddenly become vast and resplendent, and the entire assembly is golden in color!"

The Buddha answered Ānanda, "Vimalakīrti and Mañjuśrī, reverently surrounded by a great multitude, intend to come here. These auspicious signs have appeared in advance of their arrival."

At that time Vimalakīrti said to Mañjuśrī, "We can go to see the Buddha together and, along with all the Bodhisattvas, bow and make offerings to him."

Mañjuśrī said, "Excellent! Let us go! Now is the time." 11.110

Then, with his spiritual powers, Vimalakīrti placed the whole great assembly and their lion thrones in his right hand and set off for where the Buddha was. Upon arriving,

Vimalakīrti set the assembly down, bowed at the Buddha's feet, circumambulated him seven times to the right, put his palms together single-mindedly, and stood to one side. Then all the Bodhisattvas rose from their seats, bowed at the Buddha's feet, circumambulated him seven times to the right, and stood to one side. All the Śrāvakas, Śakras, brahmās, four heavenly kings, and so on likewise rose from their seats, bowed at the Buddha's feet, and stood to one side. Then the World Honored One, having greeted all the Bodhisattvas in the proper way, told each of them to be seated. Doing as the Buddha said, the assembly settled in their seats.

The Buddha then said to Śāriputra, "Did you see what these Bodhisattvas Mahāsattvas were able to do with their spiritual powers of self-mastery?"

11.111 "Yes, I did!"

"What do you think?"

"World Honored One! I think they are amazing! I cannot conceive of them; I cannot fathom them."

Then Ānanda said to the Buddha, "World Honored One! The fragrance I am smelling right now is like nothing I have ever smelled before! What is it?"

The Buddha told Ānanda, "It is the fragrance exuded from the pores of these Bodhisattvas."

Then Śāriputra said to Ānanda, "This fragrance is also emanating from our pores."

Ānanda said, "Where is it coming from?"

Śāriputra replied, "The fragrance is emanating from the pores of the people in the house, who all ate the Buddha's leftover food, which the elder Vimalakīrti brought from the land Myriad Fragrances."

Ānanda asked Vimalakīrti, "How long will this fragrance last?"

Vimalakīrti replied, "Until the food has been digested."

Ānanda asked, "How long will it be until the food has been digested?" 11.112

Vimalakīrti replied, "The power of this food is such that it will not be digested for seven days. Furthermore, Ānanda! If those Śrāvakas who have not yet ended their outflows eat this food, they will end them. Only then will the food be digested. If those who have already ended their outflows eat this food, they will attain liberation of the mind. Only then will the food be digested. If those who have not yet brought forth the resolve for the Great Vehicle eat this food, they will bring it forth. Only then will the food be digested. If those who have already brought forth the resolve eat this food, they will attain the patient acceptance of the nonarising of phenomena. Only then will the food be digested. If those who have already attained the patient acceptance of the nonarising of phenomena eat this food, they will be destined to attain Buddhahood in their next life. Only then will the food be digested. This is like the medicine 'superb flavor.' Those who take this medicine have their body purged of all poisons. Only then does the effect of the medicine end. In the same way, only when the poison of the afflictions has been eradicated will this food be digested."

Ānanda said to the Buddha, "This is unprecedented, World Honored One! This fragrant food is able to accomplish the Buddhas' work!"

The Buddha said, "Indeed, Ānanda! Indeed! There 11.113
are some Buddhalands where the brilliance of the Buddha's light accomplishes the Buddhas' work; where the myriad Bodhisattvas accomplish the Buddhas' work; where people conjured by the Buddha accomplish the Buddhas' work; where bodhi trees accomplish the Buddhas' work; where the Buddha's robes and bedding accomplish the Buddhas' work; where food accomplishes the Buddhas' work; where gardens, groves, and pavilions accomplish the Buddhas'

work; where the thirty-two hallmarks and eighty subsidiary characteristics accomplish the Buddhas' work; where the Buddha's body accomplishes the Buddhas' work; or where empty space accomplishes the Buddhas' work. In response to these conditions, living beings are led to undertake the practice of the precepts.

"There are places where dreams, illusions, shadows, echoes, reflections in a mirror, the moon's reflection in water, mirages in the heat, and other such analogies accomplish the Buddhas' work; or where sounds, language, and words accomplish the Buddhas' work. There are pure Buddhalands where tranquil silence, the absence of words, explanations, comments, and opinions, nonaction, and the unconditioned accomplish the Buddhas' work. In this way, Ānanda, there is nothing about the Buddhas' deportment, nothing in what they do, that does not accomplish the Buddhas' work.

11.114 "Ānanda! Living beings are troubled by the four demons and the eighty-four thousand afflictions; through these troubles, the Buddhas carry out their work. This is to enter the Dharma-door of all Buddhas. Bodhisattvas who enter this door do not give rise to joy, craving, or conceit when they see pure and well-adorned Buddhalands, nor do they give rise to worry, aversion, or contempt when they see impure Buddhalands. They have only pure thoughts toward all Buddhas and feel unprecedented joy and reverence.

"The merit of all Buddhas is equal. In order to teach living beings, the Buddhas manifest different Buddhalands. Ānanda! As you can see, Buddhalands vary, but empty space is everywhere the same. In the same way, the Buddhas' bodies vary, yet their unobstructed wisdom is always the same.

"Ānanda! All Buddhas' bodies, majestic hallmarks, lineage, precepts, samādhi, wisdom, liberation, knowledge and vision of liberation, [ten] powers, [four kinds of] fearlessness, [eighteen] unique attributes, great kindness, great compassion, awe-inspiring deportment, and life spans as well as their teaching of the Dharma, their bringing of living beings to perfection, their purification of Buddhalands, and their mastery of the Buddhadharma are all equal. Thus are they called Samyaksaṃbuddha, Tathāgata, and Buddha.

"Ānanda! If I were to extensively explain these three titles, you would not be able to fully understand them even if your life span were eons long. Even if the trichiliocosm were filled with living beings like you, Ānanda, all foremost in learning and possessing perfect memory, and they all had life spans eons long, they too would not be able to fully understand these titles. Therefore, Ānanda! All the Buddhas' anuttarā samyaksaṃbodhi is infinite. Their wisdom and eloquence are inconceivable."

Ānanda said to the Buddha, "From this day forward, I will never again claim that my learning is extensive."

The Buddha told Ānanda, "Do not give rise to thoughts 11.115
of retreat! Why not? When I said that you were foremost in learning among the Śrāvakas, I was not comparing you to the Bodhisattvas. Never mind, Ānanda! The wise should not try to fathom the Bodhisattvas. The depths of the ocean can be fathomed, but the merit of the Bodhisattvas' dhyāna, wisdom, dhāraṇī, and eloquence is unfathomable. Ānanda! Do not speculate about the Bodhisattvas. All Śrāvakas and Pratyekabuddhas, exerting all their powers of transformation for hundreds of thousands of eons, could not match the spiritual power that Vimalakīrti has just now displayed."

At that time the Bodhisattvas from the world Myriad Fragrances put their palms together and asked the Buddha, "World Honored One! When we first saw this land, we regarded it with contempt. Now we are ashamed and renounce such thoughts. Why? The Buddhas' skillful means are inconceivable. In order to save living beings, the Buddhas manifest various Buddhalands in response to the potentials of living beings. Indeed, World Honored One! We sincerely hope that you will bestow the Dharma upon us, so that when we return to our land, we will be mindful of the Tathāgatas."

The Buddha told the Bodhisattvas, "You must learn the Dharma-doors of liberation that has an end and liberation that does not have an end. What is meant by liberation that has an end? The conditioned. What is meant by liberation that does not have an end? The unconditioned. As Bodhisattvas, you should not completely abandon the conditioned or abide in the unconditioned.

11.116 "What is meant by not completely abandoning the conditioned?

It means not to forsake great kindness and not to renounce great compassion.
It means to bring forth a profound resolve for omniscient wisdom, never forgetting it for even a moment.
It means to teach living beings without ever growing tired.
It means to be ever mindful of the four methods of attraction and cultivate them accordingly.
It means to protect and support the Proper Dharma without concern for one's own body or life.
It means to plant good roots without ever growing weary.

It means to be firmly grounded in one's resolve and skillfully make dedications.
It means to tirelessly engage in the search for the Dharma and teach it without reserve.
It means to diligently make offerings to all Buddhas and thereby be fearless in the midst of birth and death.

It means to be free from delight and despair in the face of honor and disgrace. 11.117
It means not to disparage those not yet learned, and to revere the learned as one would revere the Buddhas.
It means to inspire those mired in affliction to bring forth proper mindfulness.
It means not to regard the bliss of seclusion as lofty.

It means, while not attaching to one's own joy, to celebrate the joy of others.
It means, while in dhyāna, to regard it as being in the hells.
It means, while in the midst of the cycle of birth and death, to regard it as a scenic garden.
It means to regard those who come to make a request as good teachers.
It means, in renouncing everything, to perfect omniscient wisdom.
It means to wish to rescue those who violate the precepts.
It means to regard the pāramitās as one's parents.
It means to regard the [thirty-seven] factors of awakening as one's relatives.
It means to set no limit on the cultivation of good roots.
It means to create one's own Buddhaland by adorning the pure lands of others.

It means to perfect one's physical features through the practice of infinite giving. 11.118
It means to purify one's body, speech, and mind by eradicating all evils.

It means to have the courage and resolve to pass through birth and death for countless eons.
It means not to become disheartened upon hearing of the Buddhas' limitless virtue.
It means to overcome the thieves of affliction with the sword of wisdom.
It means to transcend the [five] skandhas, the [eighteen] sense realms, and the [six] sense gates[40] in order to carry living beings to ultimate liberation.
It means to vanquish the demonic armies through great vigor and constantly seek the wisdom of ultimate reality that is free of thought.

11.119 It means to have few desires and know contentment with regard to worldly phenomena, to never tire of seeking the transcendent yet not forsake worldly phenomena.
It means to maintain awe-inspiring deportment yet conform to worldly custom.
It means to employ spiritual powers and wisdom to guide living beings to attain dhāraṇī, by means of which they never forget what they hear.
It means to skillfully discern all roots and sever the doubts of living beings.
It means to use eloquence in teaching others with joy to expound the Dharma without obstruction.
It means to purify the ten wholesome deeds and receive the blessing of rebirth in the heavenly and human realms.

It means to cultivate the four infinite states of mind and reveal the path to the Brahmā heavens.

It means to request the teaching of the Dharma and to rejoice in and praise the Buddhas' goodness, thereby attaining the voice of a Buddha.

It means to cultivate wholesome action in body, speech, and mind and attain the awe-inspiring deportment of a Buddha.

It means to profoundly cultivate wholesome Dharmas so that one's practice grows increasingly excellent.

It means to become a member of the Bodhisattva Sangha through the teachings of the Great Vehicle.

It means to be free from self-indulgence and never stray from the myriad forms of goodness.

"Practicing in this way, Bodhisattvas do not completely abandon the conditioned.

"What is meant by Bodhisattvas not abiding in the unconditioned? 11.120

It means to cultivate emptiness yet not regard emptiness as something to be realized.

It means to cultivate marklessness and effortlessness yet not regard marklessness and effortlessness as things to be realized.

It means to cultivate nonarising yet not regard nonarising as something to be realized.

It means to contemplate the impermanent yet never forsake one's good roots.

It means to contemplate the suffering of the world yet not detest birth and death.
It means to contemplate nonself yet never tire of teaching others.
It means to contemplate ultimate stillness yet never enter eternal stillness.
It means to contemplate seclusion yet engage one's body and mind in wholesome practices.
It means to contemplate the absence of any refuge yet take refuge in wholesome practices.
It means to contemplate the nonarising of all phenomena yet enter birth and death in order to carry living beings on one's back.

11.121 It means to contemplate the freedom from outflows yet not put an end to outflows.
It means to contemplate that there is nothing to be done yet do whatever it takes to teach living beings.
It means to contemplate emptiness and nonexistence yet not forsake great compassion.
It means to contemplate the due state of being of all phenomena yet not follow the teachings of the Lesser Vehicle.
It means to contemplate all phenomena as illusory, unreliable, without self, without agent, and without characteristics. Nevertheless, because their past vows have not been fulfilled, Bodhisattvas do not regard meritorious virtue, meditative concentration, or wisdom as empty.

"Practicing in this way, Bodhisattvas do not abide in the unconditioned.

Furthermore, because they are replete with
merit and virtue, they do not abide in the
unconditioned.
Because they are replete with wisdom, they do
not completely abandon the conditioned.

Because of their great kindness and compassion,
they do not abide in the unconditioned.
In order to fulfill their past vows, they do not
completely abandon the conditioned.

In order to gather the medicine of Dharma, they 11.122
do not abide in the unconditioned.
In order to prescribe the appropriate medi-
cine, they do not completely abandon the
conditioned.

Because they know that living beings are sick,
they do not abide in the unconditioned.
In order to put an end to the sickness of living
beings, they do not completely abandon the
conditioned.

"All Bodhisattvas, the noble ones, cultivate not completely abandoning the conditioned and not abiding in the unconditioned. These are the Dharma-doors of liberation that has an end and liberation that does not have an end. All of you must learn them!"

At that time those Bodhisattvas, feeling great joy upon hearing the Dharma, rained down all kinds of wonderful flowers of various colors and fragrances throughout the trichiliocosm as offerings to the Buddhas, Bodhisattvas, and this sūtra. Having done so, they bowed their heads at the Buddha's feet and praised this unprecedented occasion, saying, "In this land, only Śakyamuni Buddha is able to skillfully employ such expedients."

Then, having said this, they suddenly vanished and returned to their own land.

SEEING AKṢOBHYA BUDDHA

CHAPTER 12

Then the World Honored One asked Vimalakīrti, "You wish to see the Tathāgata. How do you contemplate the Tathāgata?"

Vimalakīrti replied, "I contemplate the Buddha in the same way as I contemplate my body as it really is. I contemplate that the Tathāgata does not come from the past, does not go into the future, and does not abide in the present. I do not contemplate the Tathāgata in terms of form, the thusness of form, or the nature of form. I do not contemplate the Tathāgata in terms of sense perception, cognition, mental formations, consciousness, the thusness of consciousness, or the nature of consciousness.

The Tathāgata does not arise from the four elements and is the same as emptiness. 12.123
The Tathāgata is not the aggregation of the six sense faculties, and is beyond the eyes, ears, nose, tongue, body, and mind.

The Tathāgata transcends the three realms and
has put an end to the three defilements.
The Tathāgata accords with the three doors
of liberation and is replete with the three
spiritual insights, which do not differ from
ignorance.
The Tathāgata is not of a single characteristic or
diverse characteristics, has no notion of self
or notion of others, is not free of characteristics
or attached to characteristics.
While teaching living beings, the Tathāgata is
not bound to this shore, the other shore, or
anywhere in between.
The Tathāgata contemplates ultimate stillness
yet never enters eternal stillness.

12.124 The Tathāgata is neither here nor there, and does
not take here to be here or there to be there.
The Tathāgata can neither be understood by
means of wisdom nor perceived with
discriminative thought.
The Tathāgata is neither dark nor bright, neither
with a name nor characteristics, neither
strong nor weak, neither pure nor defiled.
The Tathāgata is nowhere yet present
everywhere.
The Tathāgata is neither conditioned nor
unconditioned.
The Tathāgata is without words or teachings.
The Tathāgata is neither generous nor stingy,
neither upholds the precepts nor violates
them, is neither patient nor angry, neither
vigorous nor lax, neither concentrated nor
scattered, neither wise nor foolish.

The Tathāgata is neither honest nor deceitful, neither comes nor goes, neither enters nor exits, and is beyond all words and language.
The Tathāgata is neither a field of blessings nor not a field of blessings, neither worthy of offerings nor unworthy of offerings, neither grasping nor nongrasping, neither with characteristics nor without characteristics.

The Tathāgata is one with ultimate reality and the intrinsic nature of all phenomena. 12.125
The Tathāgata is indescribable, unfathomable, and beyond measurement.
The Tathāgata is neither great nor small, neither visible nor audible, neither perceivable nor understandable, and is free of all bondage.
The Tathāgata has the same wisdom as all living beings and does not differentiate among phenomena.
The Tathāgata loses nothing.
The Tathāgata is without defilement, without affliction, without action, without arising, without coming into being, and without ceasing to be.
The Tathāgata is without fear, without worry, without joy, without disgust, and without attachment.
The Tathāgata does not exist in the past, present, or future.
The Tathāgata cannot be described through language.

"World Honored One! The body of the Tathāgata is thus, and this is how I contemplate it. To contemplate it in this way is proper contemplation. To contemplate it in some other way would be improper contemplation."

At that time Śāriputra asked Vimalakīrti, "Where did you cease to be before you came into being here?"

Vimalakīrti replied, "Is the Dharma you have attained subject to coming into being or ceasing to be?"

Śāriputra said, "No, it is not."

12.126 "If phenomena are not subject to coming into being or ceasing to be, then why did you ask me, 'Where did you cease to be before you came into being here?' What did you mean by that? Suppose a magician conjured up men and women: would they be subject to coming into being or ceasing to be?"

Śāriputra replied, "There is no coming into being or ceasing to be. Have you not heard the Buddha say that all phenomena are illusory in nature?"

Vimalakīrti said, "Indeed! If all phenomena are illusory in nature, then why did you ask me, 'Where did you cease to be before you came into being here?' Śāriputra! Ceasing to be is illusory; things only appear to decay. Coming into being is illusory; things only appear to continue. When Bodhisattvas cease to be, they do not let the wholesome come to an end; when Bodhisattvas come into being, they do not let the unwholesome grow."

Then the Buddha said to Śāriputra, "There is a land called Wonderful Joy. The Buddha there is named Unmoving. It was in that land that Vimalakīrti ceased to be before he came into being here."

Śāriputra said, "This is unprecedented, World Honored One! This person could renounce a pure land and rejoice in coming to this place filled with hatred and peril."

12.127 Vimalakīrti asked Śāriputra, "What do you think? When the sun rises, does its light join with the darkness?"

Śāriputra replied, "No. When the sun rises, the darkness disappears."

Vimalakīrti asked, "Why does the sun travel across Jambudvīpa?"

Śāriputra replied, "It wishes to shine with brilliance and dispel the darkness."

Vimalakīrti said, "Bodhisattvas are just the same. Although they are born in impure Buddhalands, in order to transform living beings, they do not join with the foolish and the ignorant; instead, they eliminate the darkness of living beings' afflictions."

At that time the great assembly deeply yearned to 12.128
see Tathāgata Unmoving in the world Wonderful Joy, as well as his assembly of Bodhisattvas and Śrāvakas. The Buddha, knowing the thoughts of the assembly, said to Vimalakīrti, "Good man! Show to this assembly Tathāgata Unmoving in the world Wonderful Joy, as well as his assembly of Bodhisattvas and Śrāvakas. Everyone in the assembly wishes to see them."

Then Vimalakīrti thought, "I shall, without rising from my seat, bring over the world Wonderful Joy, including its Ring of Iron Mountains; its streams, creeks, valleys, rivers, seas, and springs; its Mount Sumeru and other mountains; its sun, moon, and stars; its palaces of gods, dragons, ghosts, spirits, and brahmās; its assemblies of Bodhisattvas and Śrāvakas; its cities, towns, and villages; its men and women, young and old; and even Tathāgata Unmoving, as well as his bodhi tree and wonderful lotuses, which carry out the Buddhas' work throughout the ten directions.

"On three jeweled stairways, which stretch from Jambudvīpa to the Trāyastriṃśa Heaven, gods descend to bow in respect to Tathāgata Unmoving and listen to the Dharma. The people of Jambudvīpa ascend these stairs to

Trāyastriṃśa Heaven to see the gods. This world Wonderful Joy is perfected with such limitless merit, which reaches up to the Akaniṣṭha Heaven and down to the water's edge. I will take it in my right hand like a potter's wheel, then bring it to this world as though it were a flower garland and show it to everyone in the assembly."

With this thought, Vimalakīrti entered samādhi. Manifesting his spiritual powers, he picked up the world Wonderful Joy in his right hand and put it down in this land.

12.129 The Bodhisattvas, Śrāvakas, and gods as well as those humans with spiritual powers all called out, "World Honored One! Who is taking us away? Please save us!"

Buddha Unmoving said, "This is not my doing. It is Vimalakīrti with his spiritual powers."

Those who did not have spiritual powers were completely unaware of where they had gone. Although it had been brought to this land, the world Wonderful Joy neither grew nor shrunk. Nor did it crowd this world in any way. This land remained the same. At that time Śakyamuni Buddha told the great assembly, "Look at Tathāgata Unmoving in the world Wonderful Joy. His land is magnificently adorned, the practices of his Bodhisattvas are pure, and the conduct of his disciples is pristine."

Those in the assembly said, "Yes, we see."

The Buddha said, "If Bodhisattvas wish to attain a Buddhaland of such purity, they should study the ways practiced by Tathāgata Unmoving."

When the world Wonderful Joy was made to appear, fourteen nayutas of people in the Sahā world brought forth the resolve for anuttarā samyaksaṃbodhi and vowed to be reborn in that world Wonderful Joy. Śakyamuni Buddha then made the prediction, "You shall all be born in that land." At that time, after benefiting those in this land who were meant to gain benefit,[41] Vimalakīrti sent the world Wonderful Joy back to its original place; and the entire assembly saw it return.

The Buddha asked Śāriputra, "Did you see this world Wonderful Joy and the Buddha Unmoving?" 12.130

"Yes, I saw them, World Honored One! May all living beings attain a pure land like that of Buddha Unmoving and spiritual powers like those of Vimalakīrti. World Honored One! We have already attained wholesome benefit from having seen, drawn near to, and made offerings to this person. Those living beings who hear this sūtra now or will hear it after the Buddha's nirvāṇa will also attain wholesome benefit. How much the more so those who, having heard the sūtra, bring forth faith and understanding in it, uphold, read, recite, and explain it for others, and practice according to its teachings! Those who hold this sūtra in their hands have attained a trove of Dharma treasures. Those who read and recite it, explain it to others, and practice according to its teachings will be protected and cherished by all Buddhas. It should be known that those who make offerings to such people are making offerings to the Buddhas. It should be known that the Tathāgata is present in the rooms of those who write this sūtra out. To rejoice upon hearing this sūtra is to attain omniscient wisdom. It should be known that to have faith and understanding in this sūtra—even so much as a single verse of four lines—and to explain it to others is to receive a prediction for anuttarā samyaksaṃbodhi."

THE OFFERING OF THE DHARMA

CHAPTER 13

At that time, from among the great assembly, Śakra, the god Indra, said to the Buddha, "World Honored One! Although I have heard hundreds of thousands of sūtras from the Buddha and Mañjuśrī, I have never heard of a sūtra such as this, that definitively teaches inconceivable, masterful spiritual powers and ultimate reality. According to my understanding of the Buddha's teaching, if there are living beings who hear this sūtra and believe in, understand, uphold, read, and recite it, they will certainly realize this Dharma—how much the more if they can practice accordingly. Such people have shut the door to all lower destinies and opened the door to all upper destinies. They are protected and cherished by all Buddhas. They win over all unorthodox practitioners, obliterate all demonic animosity, cultivate bodhi, settle themselves peacefully at the site of awakening, and follow the path taken by all Tathāgatas.

"World Honored One! If there are people who 13.131
uphold, read, recite, and practice according to this teaching,

my retinue and I will make offerings to them and serve them. Wherever this sūtra is—be it a village, town, city, mountain, forest, or wilderness—I will go there, together with my retinue, to receive the teaching. We shall inspire faith in those who do not yet have faith in this sūtra; and we shall protect those who have already brought forth faith in it."

The Buddha said, "Good indeed, good indeed, Śakra! I rejoice in what you said. This sūtra extensively explains the inconceivable anuttarā samyaksaṃbodhi of all Buddhas of the past, present, and future. Therefore, Śakra, if good men and women uphold, read, recite, and make offerings to this sūtra, they are making offerings to the Buddhas of the past, present, and future.

13.132 "Śakra! Suppose the trichiliocosm were filled with Buddhas numbering as many as the sugarcane, bamboo, reed, rice, hemp, and trees in a forest. Suppose there are good men or good women who, for an eon or less than an eon, venerate, praise, make offerings to, and attend to all the needs of these Buddhas until they enter parinirvāṇa. And suppose they build stūpas of the seven treasures to house the whole-body śarīra of each and every one of these Buddhas: stūpas splendidly adorned with flagpoles,[42] as long and broad as a world system and reaching up toward the Brahmā heavens. Then suppose these people, for an eon or less than an eon, make offerings of flowers, incense, jeweled necklaces, banners and pennants, and music, all of utmost subtlety and wonder. What do you think, Śakra? Will the merit these people have planted be great or not?"

Śakra, the god Indra, replied, "They would be great indeed, World Honored One! One could never finish speaking of their merit, even after hundreds of thousands of koṭis of eons."

The Buddha told Śakra, "You should know that, if these good men or women, after hearing this sūtra of inconceivable liberation, believe in, understand, uphold, read, recite, and practice it, their merit will surpass those mentioned previously. Why is that? The bodhi of all Buddhas derives from this sūtra. Because bodhi is limitless, their merit will also be limitless."

The Buddha continued, "Long ago, countless 13.133
asaṃkhyeya eons ago, there was a Buddha known as Tathāgata Medicine King, One Worthy of Offerings, One of Right and Universal Knowledge, One of Perfect Clarity and Conduct, Sugata, Knower of the World, Unsurpassed One, Subduing and Regulating Hero, Teacher of Gods and Humans, Buddha, and World Honored One. His world was called Magnificent Adornment, and his eon was called Adornment. His life span as a Buddha was twenty small eons. His Śrāvaka Sangha numbered thirty-six koṭis of nayutas, and his Bodhisattva Sangha numbered twelve koṭis.

"Śakra! At that time there was a wheel-turning sage king named Jeweled Canopy who possessed the seven treasures and ruled over one world system. This king had one thousand sons, who were upright and courageous and could subdue their bitter enemies. At that time Jeweled Canopy and his retinue made offerings to Tathāgata Medicine King and attended to all his needs for five whole eons. Afterward, he told his thousand sons, 'You should follow me in making offerings to the Buddha with deep sincerity.'

"Then his thousand sons followed their father's 13.134
instructions and made offerings to Tathāgata Medicine King for another five eons, providing for all his needs. One of his sons, whose name was Moon Canopy, sat alone and thought, 'Is there any offering superior to this?' Then, aided by the Buddha's spiritual power, a god spoke from the heavens, saying, 'Good man! The offering of the Dharma surpasses all other kinds of offerings.' Straightaway the son asked, 'What is meant by the offering of the Dharma?' The god replied, 'Go

ask Tathāgata Medicine King. He will explain the offering of the Dharma for you in detail.' At that time Prince Moon Canopy went to Tathāgata Medicine King, bowed his head at the Buddha's feet, withdrew to one side, and said to the Buddha, 'World Honored One, of all offerings, the offering of the Dharma is foremost. What is meant by the offering of the Dharma?'

13.135 "The Buddha said, 'Good man! This is what is meant by the offering of the Dharma: Suppose there are profound sūtras taught by all Buddhas. The whole world finds them difficult to believe and accept. Subtle, wonderful, rare, and pure, they cannot be understood by thought alone. They are encompassed by the Bodhisattvas' treasury of Dharma and bear the seal of dhāraṇī. They bring about the attainment of irreversibility, the perfection of the six pāramitās, the skillful discernment of principles, and accordance with the practices leading to bodhi. Surpassing all other sūtras, they result in unity with great kindness and compassion and the departure from all demonic activities and improper views. In accordance with causality, they are without self, without others, without living beings, without life span, empty, markless, effortless, and nonarising. They enable living beings to sit at the site of awakening, turn the Dharma wheel, and be venerated and praised by all gods, dragons, spirits, gandharvas, and so on.

"'They lead living beings to enter the treasury of the Buddhadharma and gather in the wisdom of all sages and worthies. They describe the path walked by all Bodhisattvas, following the principles of ultimate reality with regard to all phenomena. They clearly proclaim the Dharma of impermanence, suffering, emptiness, nonself, and ultimate stillness. They can save those living beings who violate the precepts. They frighten all demons and deviant practitioners as well as those with attachments. They are praised by all Buddhas, sages, and worthies. Leaving the suffering of birth and death behind and demonstrating the bliss of nirvāṇa, they are taught by all Buddhas of the ten directions and three periods of time. Suppose someone hears sūtras such as these, brings forth faith and understanding in them, and upholds, reads, recites, and uses skillful means to explain them to living beings in detail in order to protect the Dharma. This is what is meant by the offering of the Dharma.

"'"Furthermore, what is meant by the foremost offer- 13.136
ing of the Dharma? Cultivating according to all Dharma; investigating the twelve links of dependent arising; departing from all improper views; attaining the patient acceptance of the nonarising of phenomena; becoming firmly established in the absence of self and living beings yet not contradicting cause and effect; leaving behind self and what pertains to a self; relying on meaning instead of words; relying on wisdom instead of thought; relying on sūtras of definitive meaning instead of sūtras of provisional meaning; relying on the Dharma instead of people; and according with phenomena, in which there is nowhere to enter or return to.

"'"Ignorance is fundamentally still; therefore, volitional actions are also fundamentally still. This is the case up to and including birth being fundamentally still and therefore old age and death also being fundamentally still. Only contemplation of this kind can lead to the realization that the twelve links of dependent arising are not subject to ceasing to be or coming into being. This is what is meant by the foremost offering of the Dharma."'"

The Buddha said to Śakra, "When Prince Moon 13.137
Canopy heard this Dharma from Medicine King Buddha, he attained the patience that accords with the truth.[43] Then, removing his jeweled robe and body ornaments, he offered them to the Buddha with the words, 'World Honored One, after the Tathāgata enters nirvāṇa, I will make an offering of the Dharma as well as guard and protect the Proper

Dharma. May you, with your awe-inspiring spiritual power, compassionately aid me so that I will be able to subdue demonic resentment and cultivate Bodhisattva practices.'

"The Buddha, knowing the thoughts deep within the prince's heart, gave him this prediction: 'In the future age of the Dharma's demise, you will guard and protect the city of Dharma.' Śakra! At that time Prince Moon Canopy perceived the purity of the Dharma. Having heard the Buddha's prediction, out of faith he left the home life to cultivate all wholesome practices. Cultivating vigorously, before long he attained the five spiritual powers, realized the Bodhisattva Path, attained dhāraṇī, and gained inexhaustible eloquence.

13.138 "After that Buddha entered nirvāṇa, the prince, by means of the spiritual powers, dhāraṇī, and eloquence he had attained, turned the Dharma wheel turned by Tathāgata Medicine King for fully ten small eons. Within that very life, Bhikṣu Moon Canopy, for the sake of guarding and protecting the Dharma, practiced with diligence and vigor and transformed millions of koṭis of people so that they would never retreat from anuttarā samyaksaṃbodhi. Fourteen nayutas of people brought forth profound aspirations to become Śrāvakas or Pratyekabuddhas, and countless living beings were reborn in the heavens.

"Śakra! Was the King Jeweled Canopy of that time anyone else? Now that he has attained Buddhahood, he is known as Tathāgata Jeweled Flame; and his thousand princes will be the thousand Buddhas of the Auspicious Eon. Krakucchanda was the first of these Buddhas, and the last Tathāgata will be known as Rucika. And I was the Bhikṣu Moon Canopy of that time. Thus, Śakra, you should understand that, in essence, the offering of the Dharma is foremost, supreme, peerless, and unparalleled among all the kinds of offerings. Therefore, Śakra, you should make offerings of the Dharma to the Buddhas."

ENTRUSTMENT

CHAPTER 14

At that time the Buddha told Maitreya Bodhisattva, "Maitreya, I now entrust to you the Dharma of anuttarā samyaksaṃbodhi that I have accumulated over countless koṭis of asaṃkhyeya eons. After the Buddha's parinirvāṇa, in the future age of the Dharma's demise, you should, by means of your spiritual powers, propagate sūtras of this kind far and wide throughout Jambudvīpa and keep them in circulation. Why? In the future, there will be good men and women, gods, dragons, ghosts, spirits, gandharvas, rākṣasas, and so on who resolve on anuttarā samyaksaṃbodhi and delight in the great Dharma. If they cannot hear sūtras such as these, they will be unable to benefit from them. When such people hear sūtras of this kind, they will certainly bring forth great faith and joy, think them rare, and receive them with respect. In accord with what would benefit living beings, they will widely teach the Dharma for their sake.

"Maitreya, you should know that there are two 14.139
kinds of Bodhisattvas. What are they? The first kind delights

in works of literary elegance, while the second kind is undaunted by profound principles and can understand them as they really are. You should know that those people who delight in works of literary elegance are newly resolved Bodhisattvas. Suppose there are those who are undaunted by such profound sūtras that teach freedom from defilement and attachment and can master them. Hearing these sūtras, their minds are purified, and they are able to uphold, read, and recite them and cultivate accordingly. You should know that such Bodhisattvas have cultivated for a long time.

"Furthermore, Maitreya! There are two situations in which the newly resolved cannot set their minds on the profound Dharma. What are they? In the first case, upon hearing such profound sūtras, which they have never heard before, these people become doubtful and afraid. Unable to follow their teachings, they slander them in disbelief, saying, 'I have never heard such things before. Where do these sūtras come from?' In the second case, these people refuse to draw near, make offerings, or pay respects to those who protect and explain such profound sūtras, and may at times even speak about their faults. You should know that newly resolved Bodhisattvas who fall into these two situations are ruining themselves. They cannot bring their minds into harmony with the profound Dharma.

14.140 "Furthermore, Maitreya! There are two situations in which, although Bodhisattvas have faith and understanding in the profound Dharma, they are ruining themselves and will not be able to attain the patient acceptance of the nonarising of phenomena. What are they? In the first case, they disparage newly resolved Bodhisattvas and refuse to teach them. In the second case, they comprehend the profound Dharma yet make distinctions and then grasp at appearances on the basis of them. These are the two."

Hearing this, Maitreya Bodhisattva said to the Buddha, "World Honored One! This is unprecedented. As the Buddha said, I should distance myself from such faults and instead uphold the Dharma of anuttarā samyaksaṃbodhi accumulated by the Tathāgatas over numberless asaṃkhyeya eons. If, in the future, there are good men and good women who seek the Great Vehicle, I shall place such sūtras in their hands and empower them with the concentration to uphold, read, recite, and explain them to others far and wide. World Honored One! If, in the future age of the Dharma's demise, there are those who can uphold, read, recite, or explain these sūtras for others, this will undoubtedly be the result of my spiritual powers."

The Buddha replied, "Good indeed, good indeed, 14.141
Maitreya! The Buddhas rejoice in what you said."

Thereupon all the Bodhisattvas put their palms together and addressed the Buddha, saying, "After the Buddha's parinirvāṇa, we, too, will propagate the Dharma of anuttarā samyaksaṃbodhi far and wide throughout the lands of the ten directions. Moreover, we will guide those who teach the Dharma to comprehend these sūtras."

Then the four heavenly kings addressed the Buddha, saying, "World Honored One, wherever there are those who read, recite, or explain these sūtras to others—whether in cities, villages, forests, or the wilderness—we will lead our retinues there to listen to the Dharma. We will lend these people our support and protection, so that no one within a hundred yojanas of them will be able to seek out their weaknesses or take advantage of them."

At that time the Buddha told Ānanda, "Uphold this sūtra and propagate it far and wide."

Ānanda replied, "Certainly! I have upheld its essence. World Honored One, what shall we call this sūtra?"

The Buddha said, "Ānanda, this sūtra is entitled *The Sūtra Taught by Vimalakīrti*. It is also known as *The Inconceivable Dharma-Door of Liberation*. You should uphold it thus."

When the Buddha taught this sūtra, the elder Vimalakīrti, Mañjuśrī, Śāriputra, Ānanda, all the gods, humans, and asuras, and the rest of the great assembly, hearing what the Buddha had said, rejoiced greatly.

ENDNOTES

1. That is, ten kinds of wisdom power possessed by and unique to the Buddha:

    i. The wisdom of discerning right and wrong in every situation
    ii. The wisdom of knowing karmic results throughout the three periods of time
    iii. The wisdom of knowing all stages of dhyāna, liberation, and samādhi
    iv. The wisdom of knowing the superior and inferior potentials of living beings
    v. The wisdom of knowing the interests and inclinations of living beings
    vi. The wisdom of knowing the conditions of living beings
    vii. The wisdom of knowing the future rebirths of all living beings
    viii. The unobstructed wisdom of the heavenly eye that knows the future rebirths and deaths of living beings and their karmic reasons
    ix. The nonoutflow wisdom of knowing past lives
    x. The wisdom of knowing the permanent elimination of habitual tendencies

2. That is, the four kinds of fearlessness of a Buddha in teaching the Dharma:

    i. Fearlessness deriving from knowledge of all phenomena
    ii. Fearlessness deriving from knowledge that all outflows are destroyed
    iii. Fearlessness in explaining the impediments to awakening
    iv. Fearlessness in teaching the cessation of suffering

3. That is, the eighteen distinctive qualities unique to a Buddha:

    i. No fault in physical actions
    ii. No fault in speech

iii. No fault in mind
iv. Impartiality of mind toward all beings
v. Constant abiding in meditative concentration
vi. Complete understanding of and detachment from all phenomena
vii. Never-subsiding desire (to save living beings)
viii. Never-subsiding vigor
ix. Never-subsiding mindfulness
x. Never-subsiding wisdom
xi. Never-subsiding liberation
xii. Never-subsiding vision attained in liberation
xiii. Physical actions in harmony with wisdom
xiv. Speech in harmony with wisdom
xv. Mind in harmony with wisdom
xvi. Unobstructed wisdom of the past
xvii. Unobstructed wisdom of the future
xviii. Unobstructed wisdom of the present

4. Here, and a few stanzas below, "the Ten Powers" refers to the Buddha.

5. The complete list of the thirty-seven factors of awakening consists of seven categories:

A. The four foundations of mindfulness
i. Contemplation of the body as impure
ii. Contemplation of sense perception as suffering
iii. Contemplation of the mind as transitory
iv. Contemplation of phenomena as lacking inherent existence

B. The four kinds of right effort
i. Bringing forth latent good roots
ii. Nurturing existing good roots
iii. Preventing latent evils
iv. Eradicating existing evils

C. The four steps to spiritual powers
i. Desire
ii. Vigor
iii. Mindfulness
iv. Consideration

D. The five roots
i. Faith
ii. Vigor
iii. Mindfulness

iv. Concentration
v. Wisdom

E. The five powers
i. The power of faith
ii. The power of vigor
iii. The power of mindfulness
iv. The power of concentration
v. The power of wisdom

F. The seven factors of awakening
i. Investigation of the Dharma
ii. Vigor
iii. Joy
iv. Lightness and ease
v. Equanimity
vi. Concentration
vii. Mindfulness

G. The eightfold path
i. Right view
ii. Right thought
iii. Right speech
iv. Right action
v. Right livelihood
vi. Right effort
vii. Right mindfulness
viii. Right concentration

6. Eight conditions in which it is difficult to hear the Buddha's teaching:
i. Being born in the hells
ii. Being born as an animal
iii. Being born as a hungry ghost
iv. Being born in Uttarakuru
v. Being born in the Heaven of Long Life Span (known as Heaven of No Thought; Skt. Asajjñisattvāḥ or Asañjñisattva)
vi. Being blind, deaf, and mute
vii. Being worldly-wise
viii. Being born when there is not a Buddha in the world

7. That is, living beings who cultivate the ten wholesome deeds and receive the benefits of cultivating them. For example, speaking truthfully is one of the ten wholesome deeds, while not dying prematurely is a result of not killing.

8. According to the *Digital Dictionary of Buddhism*, the Chinese phrase 白衣 ("white-robed") "refers to secular people, who, in ancient India, wore white clothes in contrast to the darker clothes 黑衣 ['black-robed'] of religious practitioners." (http://buddhism-dict.net/cgi-bin/xpr-ddb.pl?q=%E7%99%BD%E8%A1%A3)

9. Here, Master Xuanzang's translation uses *pudgala* (Ch. 補特伽羅), a Sanskrit word meaning "individual" or "person." Master Kumārajīva simply uses the word *person* (Ch. 人).

10. This may mean that the body's movement is a result of the wind element (the 氣 *qi* or breath).

11. The twelve sense fields are also implied.

12. That is, the spiritual insight into past lives, the spiritual insight for ending outflows, and the spiritual insight of the heavenly eye.

13. The English translation follows the interpretation found in the *Weimo jingchao* 維摩經抄, which says, "The inherent nature of all phenomena refers to true thusness. The essence of all phenomena is nothing but true thusness. The awakening to true thusness is to be one with all phenomena." 《維摩經抄》卷1〈弟子品 3〉：「言法性者即真如也。法之實性莫過真如。心悟真如即是入一切法也。」

14. That is, the six sense objects: forms, sounds, scents, flavors, tangible objects, and mental objects.

15. This refers to one of the monastic rules for eating: "I will make a rounded mouthful." (*Bhikkhu Pāṭimokkha*, Sekhiya, Part Two. Translated from the Pāli by Thanissaro Bhikkhu, https://www.accesstoinsight.org/tipitaka/vin/sv/ bhikkhu-pati.html.) The Buddha probably adopted it from "the Indian way of eating by first rolling the food into a ball in the hand." (*Digital Dictionary of Buddhism*, http://buddhism-dict.net/cgi-bin/xpr-ddb.pl?q=%E6%8F%A3%E9%A3%9F.) This practice is compared to breaking apart the aggregates, about which Master Kumārajīva says, "To break apart the aggregates is to break apart the aggregation of the five skandhas. The breaking apart of the five skandhas is nirvāṇa." 《注維摩詰經》卷2〈弟子品 3〉：「壞和合者壞五陰和合也。泥洹即是五陰壞也。」(CBETA, T38, no. 1775, p. 348, b11-14)

16. Master Kumārajīva's Chinese is somewhat ambiguous here. This sentence could also mean, "Phenomena are not inherently burning, so they cannot be extinguished."

17. Also known as the eight contemplations to relinquish desires:

i. Liberation, when there is internal conception of form, by contemplating the impurity of external forms
ii. Liberation, when there is no internal conception of form, by contemplating the impurity of external forms
iii. Liberation by realizing and perfectly abiding in the pure, liberated body
iv. Liberation by realizing the sphere of infinite space
v. Liberation by realizing the sphere of infinite consciousness
vi. Liberation by realizing the sphere of nothing whatsoever
vii. Liberation by realizing the sphere of neither perception nor the absence of perception
viii. Liberation by realizing and perfectly abiding in the samādhi of cessation of sense perception and cognition

18. The contraries to the eightfold path:

i. Wrong view
ii. Wrong thought
iii. Wrong speech
iv. Wrong action
v. Wrong livelihood
vi. Wrong effort
vii. Wrong mindfulness
viii. Wrong concentration

19. Six major teachers in India during the time of Śākyamuni Buddha, whose doctrines differed from the Buddha's in various ways.

20. Refer to endnote 16. The Chinese of the two passages is almost identical. This sentence could also mean, "Phenomena are not inherently burning, so they cannot be extinguished."

21. These non-Buddhist views, attributed to different groups of śramaṇas and brāhmaṇas in India during the Buddha's time, are elaborated upon in the *Sūtra on the Brahmā's Net of Sixty-Two Views* (Ch. 梵網六十二見經, Skt. *Brahmajāla Sūtra*).

22. In his *Weimo yiji* 維摩義記, Master Huiyuan tells the following story about Ānanda fetching milk for the Buddha: "When the Buddha was in the city of Vaiśālī, there was a brāhmaṇa who, having wrong views and no faith, kept a dairy cow at his home. This cow was quick to anger and often kicked people. No one dared go near her. In order to rescue this brāhmaṇa, the Buddha manifested an illness that required him to take

cow's milk as a treatment. Ānanda took a bowl and visited the household of this brāhmaṇa to request milk from him. Seeing Ānanda, the brāhmaṇa was enraged and demanded to know what he wanted. Ānanda replied, 'The Buddha is sick and needs milk. That is why I am here.' Hearing this, the brāhmaṇa thought, 'Aha! I'll send him to get the milk; then my cow will kill him!' Then he said to Ānanda, 'You'll have to fetch the milk yourself.' To which Ānanda replied, 'Very well,' and approached the cow. She welcomed him and let him take as much milk as he wanted. She said to Ānanda, 'Please save some milk for my calf. The rest can be offered to the Buddha.' But the calf said, 'Please offer my share to the Buddha as well. I will eat grass instead.' The brāhmaṇa, standing aside and seeing all this, immediately felt ashamed and regretted what he had done. 'I cannot even compare with this cow or her calf. Not knowing the field of blessing, I gave rise to evil thoughts.' Then, going to the Buddha, he brought forth profound faith and took refuge with him. So the sūtra text says, 'Bringing living beings to liberation... he employs [skillful] means such as this.'"

23. According to Master Kumārajīva, as quoted by Master Sengzhao in his *Zhu weimojie jing*, "The true character of all phenomena is forever in stillness. So it is called 'ultimate reality.'" 《注維摩詰經》卷4〈菩薩品 4〉：「什曰。實相常定故名正位。」(CBETA, T38, no. 1775, p. 361, b21-24)

24. According to the *Digital Dictionary of Buddhism*, "The three sure or certain things that are the unchanging body 身, the true life 命 of wisdom, and the treasure 財 of enlightenment; i.e., the rewards of the true disciple—an infinite body or personality, an endless life, and boundless (spiritual) possessions, 無極之身, 無窮之命, 無盡之財. Also written as 三堅法." (http://www.buddhism-dict.net/cgi-bin/xpr-ddb.pl?q=%E5%A0%85%E6%B3%95)

25. According to Master Sengzhao's *Zhu weimojie jing*, "Those of the Two Vehicles attain the three liberations [i.e., emptiness, marklessness, and effortlessness; the last item is called 'wishlessness' in some sources], but not to the ultimate point. They stop their practice halfway, before they realize ultimate attainment. This is called premature realization. Bodhisattvas do not rejoice in this." 《注維摩詰經》卷4〈菩薩品 4〉：「二乘入三脫門不盡其極。而中路取證。謂之非時。此大士之所不樂也。」(CBETA, T38, no. 1775, p. 367, a8-10)

26. Literally, 菩提相 *puti xiang*, "the characteristic of bodhi." According to Master Sengzhao's *Zhu weimojie jing*, "In the Sanskrit original, 'the characteristic of bodhi' is known as 'the characteristic of stillness.'"

《注維摩詰經》卷4〈菩薩品 4〉：「復次梵本中。菩提相亦名寂滅相。」(CBETA, T38, no. 1775, p. 369, a15-16)

27. Refer to endnote 24.

28. The six ways that Buddhist monastics maintain harmony among themselves:

i. Seeking harmony in body in order to live together harmoniously
ii. Seeking harmony in speech in order to prevent dispute
iii. Seeking harmony in mind in order to become like-minded
iv. Seeking harmony in views in order to harmonize their understanding
v. Seeking harmony through shared precepts in order to practice together harmoniously
vi. Seeking harmony through the equal sharing of benefits

29. Regarding "premature realization," refer to endnote 25.

30. Skt. Merudhvaja. *Dhvaja* means "banner."

31. The plantain or banana "tree" is not in fact a tree but a giant herbaceous plant. Instead of a woody trunk, it has only a narrow, flimsy stem sheathed in many layers of thick leaves forming what is called a pseudostem. When these leaves are peeled away, only the soft core remains. Because of this, the plantain tree is commonly used in Buddhist sūtras as an analogy for the empty nature of things.

32. Sentient beings transmigrate through the three realms on the basis of their karma. There are seven places where their consciousnesses delight in abiding. According to the *Digital Dictionary of Buddhism,* the seven abodes of consciousness refer to the seven types of sentient beings in which consciousness is a significant phenomenon (Skt. saptavijñāna-sthitayaḥ). The list below is taken from *DDB,* with some modifications in translation:

i. "The first abode: Sentient beings constituting this abode have a variety of bodies and thoughts. Humans and some gods is the usual example of sentient beings constituting this abode. The gods are those six types belonging to the realm of desire and those in the first dhyāna heaven with the exception of those gods who arose in the first eon.
ii. The second abode: Sentient beings constituting this abode have a variety of bodies but identical thoughts. The gods who arose in the first eon is the usual example of sentient beings constituting this abode. They belong to the Heaven of Brahmā Followers

梵衆天. This heaven is the lowest of the first dhyāna heaven. These are the gods which were excluded from the first abode.

iii. The third abode: Sentient beings constituting this abode have identical bodies but a variety of thoughts. The gods in the Heaven of Ultimate Light and Purity 極光淨天 is the usual example of sentient beings constituting this abode. This heaven is the last of the three heavens in the second dhyāna heaven. Vasubandhu argues that the gods of the other two heavens (the Heaven of Limited Light 少光天 and the Heaven of Limitless Light 無量光天) of the second dhyāna heaven are also included in this abode.

iv. The fourth abode: Sentient beings constituting this abode have identical bodies and thoughts. The gods of the Heaven of Pervasive Purity 遍淨天 is the usual example of sentient beings constituting this abode. This heaven is the last of the three heavens in the third dhyāna heaven.

v. The fifth abode: Sentient beings constituting this abode have gone beyond form and thoughts. The sentient beings constituting this abode belong to the first stage of the realm of the formless, the sphere of infinite space 空無邊處.

vi. The sixth abode: Sentient beings constituting this abode have gone beyond the sphere corresponding to the previous abode. The sentient beings constituting this abode belong to the second stage of the realm of the formless, the sphere of infinite consciousness 識無邊處.

vii. The seventh abode: Sentient beings constituting this abode have gone beyond the sphere corresponding to the previous abode. The sentient beings constituting this abode belong to the third stage of the realm of the formless, the sphere of nothing whatsoever 無所有處." (http://www.buddhism-dict.net/cgi-bin/xpr-ddb.pl?4e.xml+id(%27b4e03-8b58-4f4f%27)

33. According to the *Digital Dictionary of Buddhism,* nine ordeals that Śākyamuni Buddha is said to have undergone. "They are listed in the *Treatise on the Great Perfection of Wisdom* 大智度論 and other sources:

i. At the instigation of a group of Brahmans, a beautiful woman named Sundarī spread rumors to the effect that she was having an affair with Śākyamuni.

ii. Brahmans mocked Śākyamuni when a maidservant gave him an offering of rotten rice gruel in a Brahman city.

iii. King Ajita invited Śākyamuni and five hundred disciples to his kingdom but neglected to make them any offerings. For a period of ninety days, they had nothing to eat but horse fodder.
iv. A great many members of the Śākya clan were killed by King Virūḍhaka of Kośala.
v. When Śākyamuni entered a Brahman city, the king forbade the people to make him offerings or listen to him, making it so that Śākyamuni was unable to receive alms.
vi. A Brahman woman tied a bowl to her belly under her robe and claimed that she was made pregnant by Śākyamuni.
vii. Devadatta dropped a boulder from the top of Vulture Peak in an attempt to kill the Buddha. However, it missed and only injured the Buddha's toe.
viii. Once, around the time of the winter solstice, an icy wind rose and continued to blow for eight days. Śākyamuni protected himself from the cold by wearing three robes.
ix. At the urging of Devadatta, King Ajātaśatru made some wild elephants drunk and let them loose among Śākyamuni and his disciples. However, he failed in this attempt to kill the Buddha." (http://www.buddhism-dict.net/cgi-bin/xpr-ddb.pl?4e.xml+id(%27b4e5d-60f1%27))

34. A title sometimes conferred upon eminent monks in countries where Buddhism was the state religion. These monks served as spiritual guides and advisors to the country and its leaders.

35. According to the *Digital Dictionary of Buddhism*, *ṛṣis* were, "in India, forest dwelling, world-renunciant religious practitioners. The *Lankāvatāra Sūtra* 楞伽經 mentions ten kinds of ṛṣis, including walkers on the earth, fliers, wanderers at will, into space, into the deva heavens, transforming themselves into any form, etc." (http://www.buddhism-dict.net/cgi-bin/xpr-ddb.pl?4e.xml+id(%27b4ed9%27)

36. The Sanskrit name for what in China is called the Ghost constellation. According to Master Kumārajīva, "One of the twenty-eight constellations is the Ghost constellation. This Bodhisattva was born under this constellation, so he takes its name." 《注維摩詰經》卷8〈入不二法門品 9〉：「什曰。二十八宿中鬼星名也。生時所值宿。因以為名也。」(CBETA, T38, no. 1775, p. 397, b8-9)

37. According to Master Kumārajīva, as quoted by Master Sengzhao in his *Zhu weimojie jing*, meritorious deeds that create blessings result in

rebirth in the realms of humans and gods. Unwholesome deeds that create offenses result in rebirth in the three lower realms. Neutral deeds refer to the cultivation of dhyāna, which results in rebirth in the realms of form and the formless. 《注維摩詰經》卷8〈入不二法門品 9〉：「什曰。福行欲界善行。能得樂報也。罪行十不善道。能得苦報也。無動行色無色界行。」(CBETA, T38, no. 1775, p. 398, c11-14)

38. According to Master Jizang's *Weimo jing yishu*, "The emptiness of purity and defilement is the ultimate reality. The Dharma body of all Buddhas abides alike in all lands, which are equal. There has never been either superior or inferior. Therefore, one should not have thoughts of better and worse." 《維摩經義疏》卷6〈香積品 10〉：「淨穢俱空。即是實相。平等之土。諸佛法身之所同栖。未嘗優劣。故不應起高下心。」(CBETA, T38, no. 1781, p. 980, a17-19)

39. That is, to be born into one or several of the eight difficulties. Refer to endnote 6 for a complete list.

40. That is, the six sense faculties.

41. That is, Vimalakīrti made the world Wonderful Joy appear in order to benefit certain beings whose causes and conditions were such that they would benefit from its appearance.

42. A similar context can be found in Kumārajīva's translation of the *Saddharma-puṇḍarīka Sūtra* (widely known as the *Lotus Sūtra*), where the text states,

> After my parinirvāṇa, should there be people
> Who can revere and uphold this sūtra,
> Their blessings shall be limitless,
> As described above.
> Such people will, in essence, have perfected
> The practice of making all kinds of offerings
> And will have constructed stūpas for śarīra
> Adorned with the seven treasures,
> With flagpoles high and broad.

According to the supplementary notes to the *Fahua jing sandabu buzhu* 法華經三大部補注, the *Fahua jing yaojie* 法華經要解, and the *Fahua jing dacheng* 法華經大成, flagpoles did not exist in western regions (India), but their pagodas (stūpas) had golden spires on top, from which were hung banners and flags, as from a flagpole; therefore, these poles were called *biaocha* (Ch. 表刹), "symbols of the kṣetra." The pole on a pagoda represents the area of a Buddhist monastery's landed property, which is called a *kṣetra*. *Kṣetra,* meaning "field or land," refers in many sūtras to the land over which a Buddha reigns or exercises spiritual influence.

43. According to Master Kumārajīva, those who attain this patience have realized ultimate reality, but not in a profound sense. Even still, their wisdom and faith accord with ultimate reality. According to Master Sengzhao, such people have gentle minds that accord with the truth. Because of this, they are able to realize ultimate reality. But they have not yet attained the patient acceptance of the nonarising of phenomena. 《注維摩詰經》卷10〈法供養品 13〉：「什曰。柔謂軟鈍也。於實相法未能深入。軟智軟信隨順不違。故名柔順忍也。肇曰。心柔智順堪受實相。未及無生名柔順忍。」(CBETA, T38, no. 1775, p. 417, b29-c3)

維摩詰所說經

姚秦三藏法師鳩摩羅什譯

佛國品第一

如是我聞：

一時佛在毘耶離菴羅樹園，與大比丘眾八千人俱，
菩薩三萬二千，眾所知識，大智本行，皆悉成就；
諸佛威神之所建立，為護法城，受持正法；能師子
吼，名聞十方；眾人不請，友而安之；紹隆三寶， 1.001
能使不絕；降伏魔怨，制諸外道，悉已清淨，永離
蓋纏；心常安住，無礙解脫；念、定、總持，辯才
不斷；布施、持戒、忍辱、精進、禪定、智慧及方
便力，無不具足；逮無所得，不起法忍；已能隨順，
轉不退輪；善解法相，知眾生根；蓋諸大眾，得無所
畏；功德智慧，以修其心；相好嚴身，色像第一，
捨諸世間所有飾好；名稱高遠，踰於須彌；深信堅
固，猶若金剛；法寶普照，而雨甘露；於眾言音，
微妙第一；深入緣起，斷諸邪見，有無二邊，無復
餘習；演法無畏，猶師子吼，其所講說，乃如雷震，
無有量，已過量；集眾法寶，如海導師，了達諸法 1.002
深妙之義；善知眾生往來所趣及心所行；近無等等
佛自在慧、十力、無畏、十八不共；關閉一切諸惡

趣門，而生五道以現其身；為大醫王，善療眾病，應病與藥，令得服行；無量功德皆成就，無量佛土皆嚴淨；其見聞者，無不蒙益；諸有所作，亦不唐捐；如是一切功德、皆悉具足。

1.003 其名曰：等觀菩薩、不等觀菩薩、等不等觀菩薩、定自在王菩薩、法自在王菩薩、法相菩薩、光相菩薩、光嚴菩薩、大嚴菩薩、寶積菩薩、辯積菩薩、寶手菩薩、寶印手菩薩、常舉手菩薩、常下手菩薩、常慘菩薩、喜根菩薩、喜王菩薩、辯音菩薩、虛空藏菩薩、執寶炬菩薩、寶勇菩薩、寶見菩薩、帝網菩薩、明網菩薩、無緣觀菩薩、慧積菩薩、寶勝菩薩、天王菩薩、壞魔菩薩、電德菩薩、自在王菩薩、功德相嚴菩薩、師子吼菩薩、雷音菩薩、山相擊音菩薩、香象菩薩、白香象菩薩、常精進菩薩、不休息菩薩、妙生菩薩、華嚴菩薩、觀世音菩薩、得大勢菩薩、梵網菩薩、寶杖菩薩、無勝菩薩、嚴土菩薩、金髻菩薩、珠髻菩薩、彌勒菩薩、文殊師利法王子菩薩，如是等三萬二千人。

1.004 復有萬梵天王尸棄等，從餘四天下，來詣佛所，而為聽法；復有萬二千天帝，亦從餘四天下，來在會坐；并餘大威力諸天、龍神、夜叉、乾闥婆、阿脩羅、迦樓羅、緊那羅、摩睺羅伽等，悉來會坐；諸比丘、比丘尼、優婆塞、優婆夷，俱來會坐。彼時佛與無量百千之眾，恭敬圍繞，而為說法，譬如須彌山王顯於大海，安處眾寶師子之座，蔽於一切諸來大眾。

爾時，毘耶離城有長者子，名曰寶積，與五百長者子，俱持七寶蓋，來詣佛所，頭面禮足，各以其蓋共供養佛；佛之威神，令諸寶蓋合成一蓋，遍覆三千大千世界，而此世界廣長之相，悉於中現；又此三千大千世界諸須彌山、雪山、目真隣陀山、摩訶目真隣陀山、香山、寶山、金山、黑山、鐵圍山、大鐵圍山，大海江河，川流泉源，及日月星辰、天宮、龍宮、諸尊神宮，悉現於寶蓋中；又十方諸佛，諸佛說法，亦現於寶蓋中。爾時一切大眾，覩佛神力，歎未曾有！合掌禮佛，瞻仰尊顏，目不暫捨。
長者子寶積，即於佛前，以偈頌曰： 1.005

「目淨脩廣如青蓮，心淨已度諸禪定，
久積淨業稱無量，導眾以寂故稽首。
既見大聖以神變，普現十方無量土，
其中諸佛演說法，於是一切悉見聞。
法王法力超群生，常以法財施一切，
能善分別諸法相，於第一義而不動，
已於諸法得自在，是故稽首此法王。
說法不有亦不無，以因緣故諸法生，
無我無造無受者，善惡之業亦不亡。
始在佛樹力降魔，得甘露滅覺道成， 1.006
已無心意無受行，而悉摧伏諸外道。
三轉法輪於大千，其輪本來常清淨，
天人得道此為證，三寶於是現世間。
以斯妙法濟群生，一受不退常寂然，
度老病死大醫王，當禮法海德無邊。
毀譽不動如須彌，於善不善等以慈，
心行平等如虛空，孰聞人寶不敬承。
今奉世尊此微蓋，於中現我三千界， 1.007
諸天龍神所居宮，乾闥婆等及夜叉，
悉見世間諸所有，十力哀現是化變，

眾覩希有皆歎佛，今我稽首三界尊。
大聖法王眾所歸，淨心觀佛靡不欣，
各見世尊在其前，斯則神力不共法。
1.008 佛以一音演說法，眾生隨類各得解，
皆謂世尊同其語，斯則神力不共法。
佛以一音演說法，眾生各各隨所解，
普得受行獲其利，斯則神力不共法。
佛以一音演說法，或有恐畏或歡喜，
或生厭離或斷疑，斯則神力不共法。
稽首十力大精進，稽首已得無所畏，
稽首住於不共法，稽首一切大導師，
稽首能斷眾結縛，稽首已到於彼岸，
稽首能度諸世間，稽首永離生死道。
悉知眾生來去相，善於諸法得解脫，
不著世間如蓮華，常善入於空寂行，
達諸法相無罣礙，稽首如空無所依。」

1.009 爾時，長者子寶積說此偈已，白佛言：「世尊！是五百長者子，皆已發阿耨多羅三藐三菩提心，願聞得佛國土清淨，唯願世尊說諸菩薩淨土之行！」

佛言：「善哉！寶積！乃能為諸菩薩，問於如來淨土之行。諦聽！諦聽！善思念之，當為汝說！」於是寶積及五百長者子，受教而聽。

佛言：「寶積！眾生之類是菩薩佛土。所以者何？菩薩隨所化眾生而取佛土，隨所調伏眾生而取佛土，隨諸眾生應以何國入佛智慧而取佛土，隨諸眾生應以何國起菩薩根而取佛土。所以者何？菩薩取於淨國，皆為饒益諸眾生故。譬如有人，欲於空地，造立宮室，隨意無礙；若於虛空，終不能成！菩薩如是，

為成就眾生故，願取佛國，願取佛國者，非於空也。

「寶積當知！ 1.010

直心是菩薩淨土，菩薩成佛時，不諂眾生來生其國；

深心是菩薩淨土，菩薩成佛時，具足功德眾生來生其國；

菩提心是菩薩淨土，菩薩成佛時，大乘眾生來生其國；

布施是菩薩淨土，菩薩成佛時，一切能捨眾生來生其國；

持戒是菩薩淨土，菩薩成佛時，行十善道滿願眾生來生其國；

忍辱是菩薩淨土，菩薩成佛時，三十二相莊嚴眾生來生其國；

精進是菩薩淨土，菩薩成佛時，勤修一切功德眾生來生其國；

禪定是菩薩淨土，菩薩成佛時，攝心不亂眾生來生其國；

智慧是菩薩淨土，菩薩成佛時，正定眾生來生其國； 1.011

四無量心是菩薩淨土，菩薩成佛時，成就慈悲喜捨眾生來生其國；

四攝法是菩薩淨土，菩薩成佛時，解脫所攝眾生來生其國；

方便是菩薩淨土，菩薩成佛時，於一切法方便無礙眾生來生其國；

三十七道品是菩薩淨土，菩薩成佛時，念處、正勤、神足、根、力、覺、道眾生來生其國；

迴向心是菩薩淨土，菩薩成佛時，得一切具足功德國土；

1.012 說除八難是菩薩淨土，菩薩成佛時，國土無有三惡八難；

自守戒行、不譏彼闕是菩薩淨土，菩薩成佛時，國土無有犯禁之名；

十善是菩薩淨土，菩薩成佛時，命不中夭、大富梵行、所言誠諦、常以軟語、眷屬不離、善和諍訟、言必饒益、不嫉不恚、正見眾生來生其國。

「如是，寶積！菩薩隨其直心，則能發行；隨其發行，則得深心；隨其深心，則意調伏；隨意調伏，則如說行；隨如說行，則能迴向；隨其迴向，則有方便；隨其方便，則成就眾生；隨成就眾生，則佛土淨；隨佛土淨，則說法淨；隨說法淨，則智慧淨；隨智慧淨，則其心淨；隨其心淨，則一切功德淨。是故寶積！若菩薩欲得淨土，當淨其心；隨其心淨，則佛土淨。」

1.013 爾時，舍利弗承佛威神作是念：「若菩薩心淨，則佛土淨者，我世尊本為菩薩時，意豈不淨，而是佛土不淨若此？」

佛知其念，即告之言：「於意云何？日月豈不淨耶？而盲者不見。」

對曰：「不也，世尊！是盲者過，非日月咎。」

「舍利弗！眾生罪故，不見如來佛土嚴淨，非如來咎；舍利弗！我此土淨，而汝不見。」

爾時，螺髻梵王語舍利弗：「勿作是意，謂此佛土以為不淨。所以者何？我見釋迦牟尼佛土清淨，譬如自在天宮。」 1.014

舍利弗言：「我見此土丘陵坑坎、荊蕀沙礫、土石諸山、穢惡充滿。」

螺髻梵王言：「仁者心有高下，不依佛慧，故見此土為不淨耳！舍利弗！菩薩於一切眾生，悉皆平等，深心清淨，依佛智慧，則能見此佛土清淨。」

於是佛以足指按地，即時三千大千世界，若干百千珍寶嚴飾，譬如寶莊嚴佛，無量功德寶莊嚴土，一切大眾歎未曾有！而皆自見坐寶蓮華。佛告舍利弗：「汝且觀是佛土嚴淨？」

舍利弗言：「唯然，世尊！本所不見，本所不聞，今佛國土嚴淨悉現。」

佛語舍利弗：「我佛國土常淨若此，為欲度斯下劣人故，示是眾惡不淨土耳！譬如諸天，共寶器食，隨其福德，飯色有異。如是，舍利弗！若人心淨，便見此土功德莊嚴。」

當佛現此國土嚴淨之時，寶積所將五百長者子皆得無生法忍，八萬四千人皆發阿耨多羅三藐三菩提心。佛攝神足，於是世界還復如故；求聲聞乘三萬二千天及人，知有為法皆悉無常，遠塵離垢，得法眼淨；八千比丘，不受諸法，漏盡意解。

方便品第二

爾時，毘耶離大城中有長者，名維摩詰，已曾供養無量諸佛，深植善本，得無生忍；辯才無礙，遊戲神通，逮諸總持；獲無所畏，降魔勞怨；入深法門，善於智度，通達方便，大願成就；明了眾生心之所趣，又能分別諸根利鈍，久於佛道，心已純淑，決定大乘；諸有所作，能善思量；住佛威儀，心大如海，諸佛咨嗟！弟子、釋、梵、世主所敬。欲度人故，以善方便，居毘耶離；資財無量，攝諸貧民；奉戒清淨，攝諸毀禁；以忍調行，攝諸恚怒；以大精進，攝諸懈怠；一心禪寂，攝諸亂意；以決定慧，攝
諸無智；雖為白衣，奉持沙門清淨律行；雖處居家， 2.015
不著三界；示有妻子，常修梵行；現有眷屬，常樂遠離；雖服寶飾，而以相好嚴身；雖復飲食，而以禪悅為味；若至博弈戲處，輒以度人；受諸異道，不毀正信；雖明世典，常樂佛法；一切見敬，為供
養中最；執持正法，攝諸長幼；一切治生諧偶，雖 2.016
獲俗利，不以喜悅；遊諸四衢，饒益眾生；入治政法，救護一切；入講論處，導以大乘；入諸學堂，

誘開童蒙；入諸婬舍，示欲之過；入諸酒肆，能立其志；若在長者，長者中尊，為說勝法；若在居士，居士中尊，斷其貪著；若在剎利，剎利中尊，教以忍
2.017 辱；若在婆羅門，婆羅門中尊，除其我慢；若在大臣，大臣中尊，教以正法；若在王子，王子中尊，示以忠孝；若在內官，內官中尊，化政宮女；若在庶民，庶民中尊，令興福力；若在梵天，梵天中尊，誨以勝慧；若在帝釋，帝釋中尊，示現無常；若在護世，護世中尊，護諸眾生。長者維摩詰，以如是等無量方便饒益眾生。

其以方便，現身有疾。以其疾故，國王大臣、長者居士、婆羅門等，及諸王子并餘官屬，無數千人，皆往問疾。其往者，維摩詰因以身疾，廣為說法：「諸仁者！是身無常、無強、無力、無堅、速朽之法，不可信也！為苦、為惱，眾病所集。

2.018 諸仁者！如此身，明智者所不怙；
是身如聚沫，不可撮摩；是身如泡，不得久立；
是身如燄，從渴愛生；是身如芭蕉，中無有堅；
是身如幻，從顛倒起；是身如夢，為虛妄見；
是身如影，從業緣現；是身如響，屬諸因緣；
是身如浮雲，須臾變滅；是身如電，念念不住；
是身無主，為如地；是身無我，為如火；
是身無壽，為如風；是身無人，為如水；
2.019 是身不實，四大為家；是身為空，離我我所；
是身無知，如草木瓦礫；是身無作，風力所轉；
是身不淨，穢惡充滿；
是身為虛偽，雖假以澡浴衣食，必歸磨滅；
是身為災，百一病惱；是身如丘井，為老所逼；

是身無定，為要當死；
是身如毒蛇、如怨賊、如空聚，陰界諸入所共合成。

「諸仁者！此可患厭，當樂佛身。所以者何？佛身者即法身也；從無量功德智慧生，從戒、定、慧、解脫、解脫知見生，從慈、悲、喜、捨生，從布施、持戒、忍辱、柔和、勤行精進、禪定、解脫、三昧、多聞、智慧諸波羅蜜生，從方便生，從六通生，從三明生，從三十七道品生，從止觀生，從十力、四無所畏、十八不共法生，從斷一切不善法、集一切善法生，從真實生，從不放逸生；從如是無量清淨法生如來身。諸仁者！欲得佛身、斷一切眾生病者，當發阿耨多羅三藐三菩提心。」

如是長者維摩詰，為諸問疾者，如應說法，令無數千人皆發阿耨多羅三藐三菩提心。

弟子品第三

爾時，長者維摩詰，自念：「寢疾于床，世尊大慈，寧不垂愍？」

佛知其意，即告舍利弗：「汝行詣維摩詰問疾。」

舍利弗白佛言：「世尊！我不堪任詣彼問疾。所以 3.020
者何？憶念我昔，曾於林中宴坐樹下，時維摩詰來謂我言：『唯，舍利弗！不必是坐，為宴坐也。夫宴坐者，不於三界現身意，是為宴坐；不起滅定而現諸威儀，是為宴坐；不捨道法而現凡夫事，是為宴坐；心不住內亦不在外，是為宴坐；於諸見不動，而修行三十七品，是為宴坐；不斷煩惱而入涅槃，是為宴坐。若能如是坐者，佛所印可。』時我，世尊！聞說是語，默然而止，不能加報！故我不任詣彼問疾。」

佛告大目犍連：「汝行詣維摩詰問疾。」 3.021

目連白佛言：「世尊！我不堪任詣彼問疾。所以者何？憶念我昔入毘耶離大城，於里巷中為諸居士說法。時維摩詰來謂我言：『唯，大目連！為白衣居士說法，不當如仁者所說。

夫說法者，當如法說。法無眾生，離眾生垢故；
法無有我，離我垢故；法無壽命，離生死故；
法無有人，前後際斷故；法常寂然，滅諸相故；
法離於相，無所緣故；法無名字，言語斷故；
法無有說，離覺觀故；法無形相，如虛空故；
法無戲論，畢竟空故；法無我所，離我所故；
法無分別，離諸識故；法無有比，無相待故；
法不屬因，不在緣故；法同法性，入諸法故；
3.022 法隨於如，無所隨故；法住實際，諸邊不動故；
法無動搖，不依六塵故；法無去來，常不住故；
法順空，隨無相，應無作；
法離好醜，法無增損，法無生滅，法無所歸；
法過眼耳鼻舌身心；
法無高下，法常住不動，法離一切觀行。

『唯，大目連！法相如是，豈可說乎？夫說法者，無說無示；其聽法者，無聞無得。譬如幻士，為幻人說法。當建是意，而為說法。當了眾生根有利鈍，善於知見無所罣礙，以大悲心讚于大乘，念報佛恩不斷三寶，然後說法。』維摩詰說是法時，八百居士發阿耨多羅三藐三菩提心。我無此辯，是故不任詣彼問疾。」

3.023 佛告大迦葉：「汝行詣維摩詰問疾。」

迦葉白佛言：「世尊！我不堪任詣彼問疾。所以者何？憶念我昔，於貧里而行乞，時維摩詰來謂我言：『唯，大迦葉！有慈悲心而不能普，捨豪富，從貧乞。迦葉！住平等法，應次行乞食；為不食故，應行乞食；為壞和合相故，應取揣食；為不受故，應受彼食；以空聚想，入於聚落；所見色與盲等，所聞聲與響等，所嗅香與風等，所食味不分別，受諸觸如智證，知諸法如幻相；無自性，無他性；本自不然，今則無滅。迦葉！若能不捨八邪、入八解脫，以邪相入正法；以一食施一切，供養諸佛，及眾賢聖，然後可食；如是食者，非有煩惱，非離煩惱；非入定意，非起定意；非住世間，非住涅槃。其有施者，無大福，無小福；不為益，不為損，是為正入佛道，不依聲聞。迦葉！若如是食，為不空食人之施也。』時我，世尊！聞說是語，得未曾有，即於一切菩薩，深起敬心，復作是念：『斯有家名，辯才智慧乃能如是！其誰聞此不發阿耨多羅三藐三菩提心？』我從是來，不復勸人以聲聞、辟支佛行。是故不任詣彼問疾。」

佛告須菩提：「汝行詣維摩詰問疾。」 3.024

須菩提白佛言：「世尊！我不堪任詣彼問疾。所以者何？憶念我昔，入其舍，從乞食，時維摩詰取我鉢，盛滿飯，謂我言：『唯，須菩提！若能於食等者，諸法亦等，諸法等者，於食亦等；如是行乞，乃可取食。

『若須菩提不斷婬怒癡，亦不與俱；不壞於身，而隨一相；不滅癡愛，起於明脫；以五逆相而得解脫，亦不解不縛；不見四諦，非不見諦；非得果，非不得果；非凡夫，非離凡夫法；非聖人，非不聖人；雖成就一切法，而離諸法相，乃可取食。

『若須菩提不見佛，不聞法，彼外道六師：富蘭那迦葉、末伽梨拘賒梨子、刪闍夜毘羅胝子、阿耆多翅舍 3.025

欽婆羅、迦羅鳩馱迦旃延、尼犍陀若提子等，是汝之師。因其出家，彼師所墮，汝亦隨墮，乃可取食。

『若須菩提入諸邪見，不到彼岸；住於八難，不得無難；同於煩惱，離清淨法；汝得無諍三昧，一切眾生亦得是定；其施汝者，不名福田；供養汝者，墮三惡道；為與眾魔共一手作諸勞侶，汝與眾魔，及諸塵勞，等無有異；於一切眾生而有怨心，謗諸佛、毀於法，不入眾數，終不得滅度。汝若如是，乃可取食。』

「時我，世尊！聞此語茫然，不識是何言？不知以何答？便置鉢欲出其舍。維摩詰言：『唯，須菩提！取鉢勿懼。於意云何？如來所作化人，若以是事詰，寧有懼不？』我言：『不也！』維摩詰言：『一切諸法，如幻化相，汝今不應有所懼也。所以者何？一切言說不離是相；至於智者，不著文字，故無所懼。何以故？文字性離，無有文字，是則解脫；解脫相者，則諸法也。』維摩詰說是法時，二百天子得法眼淨，故我不任詣彼問疾。」

3.026 佛告富樓那彌多羅尼子：「汝行詣維摩詰問疾。」

富樓那白佛言：「世尊！我不堪任詣彼問疾。所以者何？憶念我昔於大林中，在一樹下為諸新學比丘說法。時維摩詰來謂我言：『唯，富樓那！先當入定，觀此人心，然後說法。無以穢食置於寶器，當知是比丘心之所念，無以琉璃同彼水精。汝不能知眾生根源，無得發起以小乘法。彼自無瘡，勿傷之也；欲行大道，莫示小徑；無以大海，內於牛跡；無以日光，等彼螢火。富樓那！此比丘久發大乘心，中忘此意，如何以小乘法而教導之？我觀小乘智慧微淺，猶如盲人，不能分別一切眾生根之利鈍。』時維摩詰即入三昧，令此比丘自識宿命，曾於五百佛所植眾德本，迴向阿耨多羅三藐三菩提，即時豁然，還得本心。於是諸比丘稽首禮維摩詰足。時維摩詰因為說法，於阿耨多羅三藐三菩提不復退轉。我念聲聞不觀人根，不應說法，是故不任詣彼問疾。」

佛告摩訶迦旃延：「汝行詣維摩詰問疾。」 3.027

迦旃延白佛言：「世尊！我不堪任詣彼問疾。所以者何？憶念昔者，佛為諸比丘略說法要，我即於後，敷演其義，謂無常義、苦義、空義、無我義、寂滅義。時維摩詰來謂我言：『唯，迦旃延！無以生滅心行，說實相法。迦旃延！諸法畢竟不生不滅，是無常義；五受陰，洞達空無所起，是苦義；諸法究竟無所有，是空義；於我、無我而不二，是無我義；法本不然，今則無滅，是寂滅義。』說是法時，彼諸比丘心得解脫。故我不任詣彼問疾。」

佛告阿那律：「汝行詣維摩詰問疾。」 3.028

阿那律白佛言：「世尊！我不堪任詣彼問疾。所以者何？憶念我昔於一處經行，時有梵王，名曰嚴淨，與萬梵俱，放淨光明，來詣我所，稽首作禮問我言：『幾何阿那律天眼所見？』我即答言：『仁者！吾見此釋迦牟尼佛土三千大千世界，如觀掌中菴摩勒果。』時維摩詰來謂我言：『唯，阿那律！天眼所見，為作相耶？無作相耶？假使作相，則與外道五通等；若無作相，即是無為，不應有見。』世尊！我時默然。彼諸梵聞其言，得未曾有！即為作禮而問曰：『世孰有真天眼者？』維摩詰言：『有佛、世尊，得真天眼，常在三昧，悉見諸佛國，不以二相。』於是嚴淨梵王及其眷屬五百梵天，皆發阿耨多羅三藐三菩提心，禮維摩詰足已，忽然不現！故我不任詣彼問疾。」

3.029 佛告優波離：「汝行詣維摩詰問疾。」

優波離白佛言：「世尊！我不堪任詣彼問疾。所以者何？憶念昔者，有二比丘犯律行，以為恥，不敢問佛，來問我言：『唯，優波離！我等犯律，誠以為恥，不敢問佛，願解疑悔，得免斯咎！』我即為其如法解說。時維摩詰來謂我言：『唯，優波離！無重增此二比丘罪！當直除滅，勿擾其心。所以者何？彼罪性不在內、不在外、不在中間，如佛所說，心垢故眾生垢，心淨故眾生淨。心亦不在內、不在外、不在中間，如其心然，罪垢亦然，諸法亦然，不出於如。如優波離，以心相得解脫時，寧有垢不？』我言：『不也！』維摩詰言：『一切眾生，心相無垢，亦復如是。唯，優波離！妄想是垢，無妄想是淨；顛倒是垢，無顛倒是淨；取我是垢，不取我是淨。優波離！一切法生滅不住，如幻如電，諸法不相待，乃至一念不住；諸法皆妄見，如夢、如燄、如水中月、如鏡中像，以妄想生。其知此者，是名奉律；其知此者，是名善解。』於是二比丘言：『上智哉！是優波離所不能及，持律之上而不能說。』我即答言：『自捨如來，未有聲聞及菩薩，能制其樂說之辯，其智慧明達，為若此也！』時二比丘疑悔即除，發阿耨多羅三藐三菩提心，作是願言：『令一切眾生皆得是辯。』故我不任詣彼問疾。」

3.030 佛告羅睺羅：「汝行詣維摩詰問疾。」

羅睺羅白佛言：「世尊！我不堪任詣彼問疾。所以者何？憶念昔時，毘耶離諸長者子來詣我所，稽首作禮，問我言：『唯，羅睺羅！汝佛之子，捨轉輪王位，出家為道。其出家者，有何等利？』我即如法為說出家功德之利。時維摩詰來謂我言：『唯，羅睺羅！不應說出家功德之利。所以者何？無利無功德，是為出家；有為法者，可說有利有功德。夫
出家者，為無為法，無為法中，無利無功德。羅睺 3.031
羅！出家者，無彼無此，亦無中間；離六十二見，處於涅槃；智者所受，聖所行處；降伏眾魔，度五道，淨五眼，得五力，立五根；不惱於彼，離眾雜惡；摧諸外道，超越假名；出淤泥，無繫著；無我所，無所受；無擾亂，內懷喜；護彼意，隨禪定，離眾過。若能如是，是真出家。』於是維摩詰語諸長者子：『汝等於正法中，宜共出家。所以者何？佛世難值！』諸長者子言：『居士！我聞佛言，父母不聽，不得出家。』維摩詰言：『然！汝等便發阿耨多羅三藐三菩提心，是即出家，是即具足。』爾時三十二長者子，皆發阿耨多羅三藐三菩提心，故我不任詣彼問疾。」

佛告阿難：「汝行詣維摩詰問疾。」 3.032

阿難白佛言：「世尊！我不堪任詣彼問疾。所以者何？憶念昔時，世尊身小有疾，當用牛乳，我即持鉢，詣大婆羅門家門下立。時維摩詰來謂我言：『唯，阿難！何為晨朝，持鉢住此？』我言：『居士！世尊身小有疾，當用牛乳，故來至此。』維摩詰言：『止，止！阿難！莫作是語！如來身者，金剛之體，諸惡已斷，眾善普會，當有何疾？當有何惱？默往，阿難！勿謗如來，莫使異人聞此麤言；無令大威德諸天，及他方淨土諸來菩薩得聞斯語。

阿難！轉輪聖王，以少福故，尚得無病，豈況如來無量福慧普勝者哉！行矣，阿難！勿使我等受斯恥也。外道、梵志，若聞此語，當作是念：「何名為師？自疾不能救，而能救諸疾人？」可密速去，勿使人聞。當知，阿難！諸如來身，即是法身，非思欲身。佛為世尊，過於三界；佛身無漏，諸漏已盡；佛身無為，不墮諸數。如此之身，當有何疾？當有何惱？』時我，世尊！實懷慚愧，得無近佛而謬聽耶！即聞空中聲曰：『阿難！如居士言。但為佛出五濁惡世，現行斯法，度脫眾生。行矣，阿難！取乳勿慚。』世尊！維摩詰智慧辯才，為若此也。是故不任詣彼問疾。」

如是五百大弟子，各各向佛說其本緣，稱述維摩詰所言，皆曰：「不任詣彼問疾！」

菩薩品第四

於是佛告彌勒菩薩：「汝行詣維摩詰問疾。」

彌勒白佛言：「世尊！我不堪任詣彼問疾。所以者何？憶念我昔為兜率天王及其眷屬，說不退轉地之行。時維摩詰來謂我言：『彌勒！世尊授仁者記，一生當得阿耨多羅三藐三菩提。為用何生，得受記乎？過去耶？未來耶？現在耶？若過去生，過去生已滅；若未來生，未來生未至；若現在生，現在生無住。如佛所說：「比丘！汝今即時，亦生亦老亦滅。」若以無生得受記者，無生即是正位，於正位 4.033
中，亦無受記，亦無得阿耨多羅三藐三菩提，云何彌勒受一生記乎？為從如生得受記耶？為從如滅得受記耶？若以如生得受記者，如無有生；若以如滅得受記者，如無有滅。一切眾生皆如也，一切法亦如也，眾聖賢亦如也，至於彌勒亦如也。若彌勒得受記者，一切眾生亦應受記。所以者何？夫如者不二不異，若彌勒得阿耨多羅三藐三菩提者，一切眾生皆亦應得。所以者何？一切眾生即菩提相。若彌勒得滅度者，一切眾生亦應滅度。所以者何？諸佛知一切眾生畢竟寂滅，即涅槃相，不復更滅。是故，彌勒！無以此法誘諸天子，實無發阿耨多羅三藐三
4.034 菩提心者，亦無退者。彌勒！當令此諸天子，捨於分別菩提之見。所以者何？菩提者不可以身得，不可以心得；

寂滅是菩提，滅諸相故；
不觀是菩提，離諸緣故；
不行是菩提，無憶念故；斷是菩提，捨諸見故；
離是菩提，離諸妄想故；障是菩提，障諸願故；
4.035 不入是菩提，無貪著故；順是菩提，順於如故；
住是菩提，住法性故；至是菩提，至實際故；
不二是菩提，離意法故；等是菩提，等虛空故；
無為是菩提，無生住滅故；
知是菩提，了眾生心行故；
不會是菩提，諸入不會故；
不合是菩提，離煩惱習故；
無處是菩提，無形色故；
假名是菩提，名字空故。
如化是菩提，無取捨故；
無亂是菩提，常自靜故；
善寂是菩提，性清淨故；
無取是菩提，離攀緣故；
無異是菩提，諸法等故；
無比是菩提，無可喻故；
微妙是菩提，諸法難知故。』

「世尊！維摩詰說是法時，二百天子得無生法忍。故我不任詣彼問疾。」

佛告光嚴童子：「汝行詣維摩詰問疾。」 4.036

光嚴白佛言：「世尊！我不堪任詣彼問疾。所以者何？憶念我昔出毘耶離大城，時維摩詰方入城，我即為作禮而問言：『居士從何所來？』答我言：『吾從道場來。』我問：『道場者何所是？』答曰：

『直心是道場，無虛假故；發行是道場，能辦事故；深心是道場，增益功德故；菩提心是道場，無錯謬故；

布施是道場，不望報故；持戒是道場，得願具故；忍辱是道場，於諸眾生心無礙故；精進是道場，不懈退故；禪定是道場，心調柔故；智慧是道場，現見諸法故；

慈是道場，等眾生故；悲是道場，忍疲苦故； 4.037
喜是道場，悅樂法故；捨是道場，憎愛斷故；

神通是道場，成就六通故；解脫是道場，能背捨故；方便是道場，教化眾生故；四攝是道場，攝眾生故；多聞是道場，如聞行故；伏心是道場，正觀諸法故；

三十七品是道場，捨有為法故；諦是道場，不誑世間故；緣起是道場，無明乃至老死皆
無盡故；諸煩惱是道場，知如實故；眾生是 4.038
道場，知無我故；一切法是道場，知諸法空故；降魔是道場，不傾動故；三界是道場，無所趣故；

師子吼是道場，無所畏故；力、無畏、不共法是道場，無諸過故；三明是道場，無餘礙故；一念知一切法是道場，成就一切智故。

『如是，善男子！菩薩若應諸波羅蜜教化眾生，諸有所作，舉足下足，當知皆從道場來，住於佛法矣！』說是法時，五百天、人皆發阿耨多羅三藐三菩提心。故我不任詣彼問疾。」

4.039 佛告持世菩薩：「汝行詣維摩詰問疾。」

持世白佛言：「世尊！我不堪任詣彼問疾。所以者何？憶念我昔，住於靜室，時魔波旬，從萬二千天女，狀如帝釋，鼓樂絃歌，來詣我所。與其眷屬，稽首我足，合掌恭敬，於一面立。我意謂是帝釋，而語之言：『善來憍尸迦！雖福應有，不當自恣。當觀五欲無常，以求善本，於身命財而修堅法。』即語我言：『正士！受是萬二千天女，可備掃灑。』我言：『憍尸迦！無以此非法之物要我沙門釋子，此非我宜。』所言未訖，時維摩詰來謂我言：『非帝釋也，是為魔來嬈固汝耳！』即語魔言：『是諸女等，可以與我，如我應受。』魔即驚懼，念：『維摩詰將無惱我？』欲隱形去，而不能隱；盡其神力，亦不得去。即聞空中聲曰：『波旬！以女與之，乃可得去。』魔以畏故，俛仰而與。

4.040 「爾時，維摩詰語諸女言：『魔以汝等與我，今汝皆當發阿耨多羅三藐三菩提心。』即隨所應而為說法，令發道意。復言：『汝等已發道意，有法樂可以自娛，不應復樂五欲樂也。』天女即問：『何謂法樂？』答言：『樂常信佛，樂欲聽法，樂供養眾，樂離五欲；樂觀五陰如怨賊，樂觀四大如毒蛇，樂觀內入如空聚；樂隨護道意，樂饒益眾生，樂敬養師；樂廣行施，樂堅持戒，樂忍辱柔和，樂勤集善根，
4.041 樂禪定不亂，樂離垢明慧；樂廣菩提心，樂降伏眾魔，樂斷諸煩惱，樂淨佛國土，樂成就相好故，修

諸功德；樂莊嚴道場；樂聞深法不畏；樂三脫門，不樂非時；樂近同學，樂於非同學中，心無恚礙；樂將護惡知識，樂親近善知識；樂心喜清淨，樂修無量道品之法。是為菩薩法樂。』

「於是波旬告諸女言：『我欲與汝俱還天宮。』諸女言：『以我等與此居士，有法樂，我等甚樂，不復樂五欲樂也。』魔言：『居士可捨此女？一切所有施於彼者，是為菩薩。』維摩詰言：『我已捨矣！汝便將去，令一切眾生得法願具足。』於是諸女問維摩詰：『我等云何，止於魔宮？』維摩詰言：『諸 4.042
姊！有法門名無盡燈，汝等當學。無盡燈者，譬如一燈，燃百千燈，冥者皆明，明終不盡。如是，諸姊！夫一菩薩開導百千眾生，令發阿耨多羅三藐三菩提心，於其道意亦不滅盡，隨所說法，而自增益一切善法，是名無盡燈也。汝等雖住魔宮，以是無盡燈，令無數天子天女，發阿耨多羅三藐三菩提心者，為報佛恩，亦大饒益一切眾生。』爾時天女頭面禮維摩詰足，隨魔還宮，忽然不現。世尊！維摩詰有如是自在神力，智慧辯才，故我不任詣彼問疾。」

佛告長者子善德：「汝行詣維摩詰問疾。」 4.043

善德白佛言：「世尊！我不堪任詣彼問疾。所以者何？憶念我昔，自於父舍，設大施會，供養一切沙門、婆羅門，及諸外道、貧窮、下賤、孤獨、乞人。期滿七日，時維摩詰來入會中，謂我言：『長者子！夫大施會，不當如汝所設，當為法施之會，何用是財施會為？』我言：『居士！何謂法施之會？』答曰：『法施會者，無前無後，一時供養一切眾生，是名法施之會。』曰：『何謂也？』

『謂以菩提，起於慈心；以救眾生，起大悲心；以持正法，起於喜心；以攝智慧，行於捨心；
以攝慳貪，起檀波羅蜜；以化犯戒，起尸羅波羅蜜；以無我法，起羼提波羅蜜；以離身心相，起毘梨耶波羅蜜；以菩提相，起禪波羅蜜；以一切智，起般若波羅蜜。
4.044 教化眾生，而起於空；不捨有為法，而起無相；
示現受生，而起無作；護持正法，起方便力；
以度眾生，起四攝法；以敬事一切，起除慢法；
於身命財，起三堅法；於六念中，起思念法；
於六和敬，起質直心；正行善法，起於淨命；
心淨歡喜，起近賢聖；不憎惡人，起調伏心；
以出家法，起於深心；以如說行，起於多聞；
以無諍法，起空閑處；趣向佛慧，起於宴坐；
4.045 解眾生縛，起修行地；
以具相好，及淨佛土，起福德業；
知一切眾生心念，如應說法，起於智業；
知一切法，不取不捨，入一相門，起於慧業；
斷一切煩惱、一切障礙、一切不善法，起一切善業；
以得一切智慧、一切善法，起於一切助佛道法。

『如是，善男子！是為法施之會。若菩薩住是法施會者，為大施主，亦為一切世間福田。』

「世尊！維摩詰說是法時，婆羅門眾中二百人，皆發阿耨多羅三藐三菩提心。我時心得清淨，歎未曾有！稽首禮維摩詰足，即解瓔珞價直百千而以上之，不肯
4.046 取。我言：『居士！願必納受，隨意所與。』維摩詰乃受瓔珞，分作二分，持一分施此會中一最下乞

人，持一分奉彼難勝如來。一切眾會皆見光明國土難勝如來，又見珠瓔在彼佛上變成四柱寶臺，四面嚴飾，不相障蔽。時維摩詰現神變已，又作是言：『若施主等心施一最下乞人，猶如如來福田之相，無所分別，等于大悲，不求果報，是則名曰具足法施。』城中一最下乞人，見是神力，聞其所說，皆發阿耨多羅三藐三菩提心，故我不任詣彼問疾。」

如是諸菩薩各各向佛說其本緣，稱述維摩詰所言，皆曰：「不任詣彼問疾！」

文殊師利問疾品第五

爾時，佛告文殊師利：「汝行詣維摩詰問疾。」

文殊師利白佛言：「世尊！彼上人者，難為詶對。深達實相，善說法要，辯才無滯，智慧無礙；一切菩薩法式悉知，諸佛祕藏無不得入；降伏眾魔，遊戲神通，其慧方便，皆已得度。雖然，當承佛聖旨，詣彼問疾。」

於是眾中諸菩薩、大弟子、釋、梵、四天王等，咸作是念：「今二大士，文殊師利、維摩詰共談，必說妙法！」即時八千菩薩、五百聲聞、百千天、人皆欲隨從。於是文殊師利與諸菩薩、大弟子眾，及諸天、人，恭敬圍繞，入毘耶離大城。

爾時，長者維摩詰心念：「今文殊師利，與大眾俱 5.047
來！」即以神力，空其室內，除去所有，及諸侍者；唯置一床，以疾而臥。

文殊師利，既入其舍，見其室空，無諸所有，獨寢一床。時維摩詰言：「善來，文殊師利！不來相而來，不見相而見。」

文殊師利言：「如是！居士！若來已，更不來；若去已，更不去。所以者何？來者無所從來，去者無所至，所可見者，更不可見。且置是事，居士！是疾寧可忍不？療治有損，不至增乎！世尊慇懃，致問無量，居士是疾，何所因起？其生久如？當云何滅？」

維摩詰言：「從癡有愛，則我病生。以一切眾生病，是故我病；若一切眾生病滅，則我病滅。所以者何？菩薩為眾生故入生死，有生死則有病；若眾生得離病者，則菩薩無復病。譬如長者，唯有一子，其子得病，父母亦病。若子病愈，父母亦愈。菩薩如是，於諸眾生，愛之若子；眾生病則菩薩病，眾生病愈，菩薩亦愈。又言是疾，何所因起？菩薩病者，以大悲起。」

5.048 文殊師利言：「居士此室，何以空無侍者？」

維摩詰言：「諸佛國土亦復皆空。」

又問：「以何為空？」

答曰：「以空空。」

又問：「空何用空？」

答曰：「以無分別空故空。」

又問：「空可分別耶？」

答曰：「分別亦空。」

又問：「空當於何求？」

答曰：「當於六十二見中求。」

又問：「六十二見當於何求？」

答曰：「當於諸佛解脫中求。」

又問：「諸佛解脫當於何求？」

答曰：「當於一切眾生心行中求。又仁所問：『何無侍者？』一切眾魔及諸外道，皆吾侍也。所以者何？眾魔者樂生死，菩薩於生死而不捨；外道者樂諸見，菩薩於諸見而不動。」

文殊師利言：「居士所疾，為何等相？」

維摩詰言：「我病無形不可見。」

又問：「此病身合耶？心合耶？」 5.049

答曰：「非身合，身相離故；亦非心合，心如幻故。」

又問：「地大、水大、火大、風大，於此四大，何大之病？」

答曰：「是病非地大，亦不離地大；水、火、風大，亦復如是。而眾生病，從四大起，以其有病，是故我病。」

爾時文殊師利問維摩詰言：「菩薩應云何慰喻有疾菩薩？」

維摩詰言：「說身無常，不說厭離於身；說身有苦，不說樂於涅槃；說身無我，而說教導眾生；說身空寂，不說畢竟寂滅；說悔先罪，而不說入於過去；以己之疾，愍於彼疾；當識宿世無數劫苦，當念饒益一切眾生；憶所修福，念於淨命，勿生憂惱，常起精進；當作醫王，療治眾病。菩薩應如是慰喻有疾菩薩，令其歡喜。」

文殊師利言：「居士！有疾菩薩云何調伏其心？」

5.050 維摩詰言：「有疾菩薩，應作是念：『今我此病，皆從前世妄想顛倒諸煩惱生，無有實法，誰受病者！所以者何？四大合故，假名為身；四大無主，身亦無我；又此病起，皆由著我。是故於我，不應生著。』既知病本，即除我想及眾生想。當起法想，應作是念：『但以眾法，合成此身；起唯法起，滅唯法滅。又此法者，各不相知，起時不言我起，滅時不
5.051 言我滅。』彼有疾菩薩，為滅法想，當作是念：『此法想者，亦是顛倒，顛倒者是即大患，我應離之。』云何為離？離我、我所。云何離我、我所？謂離二法。云何離二法？謂不念內外諸法行於平等。云何平等？謂我等、涅槃等。所以者何？我及涅槃，此二皆空。以何為空？但以名字故空。如此二法，無決定性，得是平等；無有餘病，唯有空病；空病亦空。是有疾菩薩以無所受而受諸受，未具佛法，亦不滅受而取證也。

5.052 「設身有苦，念惡趣眾生，起大悲心，我既調伏，亦當調伏一切眾生；但除其病，而不除法，為斷病本而教導之。何謂病本？謂有攀緣，從有攀緣，則為病本。何所攀緣？謂之三界。云何斷攀緣？以無所得，若無所得，則無攀緣。何謂無所得？謂離二見。何謂二見？謂內見外見，是無所得。文殊師利！是為有疾菩薩調伏其心，為斷老病死苦，是菩薩菩提。若不如是，己所修治，為無惠利。譬如勝怨，乃可為勇。如是兼除老病死者，菩薩之謂也。

「彼有疾菩薩，應復作是念：『如我此病，非真非有，眾生病亦非真非有。』作是觀時，於諸眾生若起愛見大悲，即應捨離。所以者何？菩薩斷除客塵煩惱而起大悲。愛見悲者，則於生死有疲厭心。若能離此，無有疲厭，在在所生，不為愛見之所覆也。所生無縛，能為眾生說法解縛，如佛所說：『若自有縛，能解彼縛，無有是處！若自無縛，能解彼縛，斯有是處。』是故菩薩不應起縛。

「何謂縛？何謂解？貪著禪味，是菩薩縛；以方便 5.053
生，是菩薩解。又無方便慧縛，有方便慧解；無慧方便縛，有慧方便解。

「何謂無方便慧縛？謂菩薩以愛見心莊嚴佛土、成就眾生；於空、無相、無作法中，而自調伏，是名無方便慧縛。

「何謂有方便慧解？謂不以愛見心莊嚴佛土、成就眾生，於空、無相、無作法中，以自調伏，而不疲厭，是名有方便慧解。

「何謂無慧方便縛？謂菩薩住貪欲、瞋恚、邪見等 5.054
諸煩惱，而植眾德本，是名無慧方便縛。

「何謂有慧方便解？謂離諸貪欲、瞋恚、邪見等諸煩惱，而植眾德本；迴向阿耨多羅三藐三菩提，是名有慧方便解。

「文殊師利！彼有疾菩薩，應如是觀諸法，又復觀身無常、苦、空、非我，是名為慧；雖身有疾，常在生死，饒益一切，而不厭倦，是名方便。又復觀身，身不離病，病不離身，是病是身，非新非故，是名為慧；設身有疾，而不永滅，是名方便。

「文殊師利！有疾菩薩應如是調伏其心，不住其中，亦復不住不調伏心。所以者何？若住不調伏心，是愚人法；若住調伏心，是聲聞法。是故菩薩不當住於調伏、不調伏心，離此二法，是菩薩行。

5.055 在於生死，不為污行；住於涅槃，不永滅度，是菩薩行；
非凡夫行，非賢聖行，是菩薩行；
非垢行，非淨行，是菩薩行；
雖過魔行，而現降眾魔，是菩薩行；
求一切智，無非時求，是菩薩行；
雖觀諸法不生，而不入正位，是菩薩行；
雖觀十二緣起，而入諸邪見，是菩薩行；
雖攝一切眾生，而不愛著，是菩薩行；
雖樂遠離，而不依身心盡，是菩薩行；
雖行三界，而不壞法性，是菩薩行；
5.056 雖行於空，而植眾德本，是菩薩行；
雖行無相，而度眾生，是菩薩行；
雖行無作，而現受身，是菩薩行；
雖行無起，而起一切善行，是菩薩行；
雖行六波羅蜜，而遍知眾生心、心數法，是菩薩行；
雖行六通，而不盡漏，是菩薩行；
雖行四無量心，而不貪著生於梵世，是菩薩行；
雖行禪定解脫三昧，而不隨禪生，是菩薩行；
5.057 雖行四念處，而不永離身受心法，是菩薩行；
雖行四正勤，而不捨身心精進，是菩薩行；
雖行四如意足，而得自在神通，是菩薩行；
雖行五根，而分別眾生諸根利鈍，是菩薩行；
雖行五力，而樂求佛十力，是菩薩行；

雖行七覺分，而分別佛之智慧，是菩薩行；
雖行八聖道，而樂行無量佛道，是菩薩行；
雖行止觀助道之法，而不畢竟墮於寂滅，是菩薩行； 5.058
雖行諸法不生不滅，而以相好莊嚴其身，是菩薩行；
雖現聲聞、辟支佛威儀，而不捨佛法，是菩薩行；
雖隨諸法究竟淨相，而隨所應為現其身，是菩薩行；
雖觀諸佛國土永寂如空，而現種種清淨佛土，是菩薩行；
雖得佛道轉于法輪，入於涅槃，而不捨於菩薩之道，是菩薩行。」

說是語時，文殊師利所將大眾，其中八千天子，皆發阿耨多羅三藐三菩提心。

不思議品第六

爾時，舍利弗見此室中無有床座，作是念：「斯諸菩薩、大弟子眾，當於何坐？」

長者維摩詰知其意，語舍利弗言：「云何仁者！為法來耶？求床座耶？」

舍利弗言：「我為法來，非為床座。」

維摩詰言：「唯，舍利弗！夫求法者，不貪軀命，何況床座？夫求法者，非有色、受、想、行、識之
求，非有界、入之求，非有欲、色、無色之求。唯， 6.059
舍利弗！夫求法者，不著佛求，不著法求，不著眾求；夫求法者，無見苦求，無斷集求，無造盡證、修道之求。所以者何？法無戲論，若言我當見苦、斷集、證滅、修道，是則戲論，非求法也。

唯，舍利弗！法名寂滅，若行生滅，是求生 6.060
滅，非求法也；
法名無染，若染於法，乃至涅槃，是則染著，非求法也；

法無行處，若行於法，是則行處，非求法也；
法無取捨，若取捨法，是則取捨，非求法也；
法無處所，若著處所，是則著處，非求法也；
法名無相，若隨相識，是則求相，非求法也；
法不可住，若住於法，是則住法，非求法也；
法不可見、聞、覺知，若行見、聞、覺知，是則見、聞、覺知，非求法也；
法名無為，若行有為，是求有為，非求法也。

是故，舍利弗！若求法者，於一切法，應無所求。」

6.061 說是語時，五百天子於諸法中，得法眼淨。

爾時，長者維摩詰，問文殊師利：「仁者遊於無量千萬億阿僧祇國，何等佛土有好上妙功德成就師子之座？」

文殊師利言：「居士！東方度三十六恒河沙國，有世界名須彌相，其佛號須彌燈王，今現在。彼佛身長八萬四千由旬，其師子座高八萬四千由旬，嚴飾第一。」

於是長者維摩詰現神通力，即時彼佛遣三萬二千師子座，高廣嚴淨，來入維摩詰室，諸菩薩、大弟子、釋、梵、四天王等，昔所未見。其室廣博，悉皆包容三萬二千師子座，無所妨礙。於毘耶離城，及閻浮提四天下，亦不迫迮，悉見如故。

6.062 爾時，維摩詰語文殊師利：「就師子座。與諸菩薩上人俱坐，當自立身如彼座像。」其得神通菩薩，即自變形為四萬二千由旬，坐師子座。諸新發意菩薩及大弟子，皆不能昇。

爾時，維摩詰語舍利弗：「就師子座。」舍利弗言：「居士！此座高廣，吾不能昇。」

維摩詰言：「唯，舍利弗！為須彌燈王如來作禮，乃可得坐。」於是新發意菩薩及大弟子，即為須彌燈王如來作禮，便得坐師子座。

舍利弗言：「居士！未曾有也，如是小室，乃容受此高廣之座，於毘耶離城，無所妨礙，又於閻浮提聚落、城邑，及四天下諸天、龍王、鬼神宮殿，亦不迫迮。」

維摩詰言：「唯，舍利弗！諸佛菩薩，有解脫，名 6.063
不可思議。若菩薩住是解脫者，以須彌之高廣內芥子中，無所增減，須彌山王本相如故，而四天王、忉利諸天，不覺不知己之所入，唯應度者乃見須彌入芥子中，是名不可思議解脫法門。又以四大海水入一毛孔，不嬈魚、鼈、黿、鼉水性之屬，而彼大海本相如故，諸龍、鬼神、阿修羅等，不覺不知己之所入，於此眾生亦無所嬈。又舍利弗！住不可思議解脫菩薩，斷取三千大千世界，如陶家輪，著右掌中，擲過恒河沙世界之外，其中眾生，不覺不知己之所往。又復還置本處，都不使人有往來想，而
此世界本相如故。又舍利弗！或有眾生，樂久住世， 6.064
而可度者，菩薩即延七日以為一劫，令彼眾生謂之一劫；或有眾生，不樂久住，而可度者，菩薩即促一劫以為七日，令彼眾生謂之七日。

「又舍利弗！住不可思議解脫菩薩，以一切佛土嚴飾之事，集在一國，示於眾生。又菩薩以一佛土眾生置之右掌，飛到十方遍示一切，而不動本處。又舍利弗！十方眾生供養諸佛之具，菩薩於一毛孔，

皆令得見。又十方國土所有日、月、星宿，於一毛孔普使見之。又舍利弗！十方世界所有諸風，菩薩悉能吸著口中，而身無損，外諸樹木，亦不摧折。又十方世界劫盡燒時，以一切火內於腹中，火事如故，而不為害。
6.065 又於下方過恒河沙等諸佛世界，取一佛土，舉著上方，過恒河沙無數世界，如持鍼鋒舉一棗葉，而無所嬈。又舍利弗！住不可思議解脫菩薩，能以神通現作佛身，或現辟支佛身，或現聲聞身，或現帝釋身，或現梵王身，或現世主身，或現轉輪王身。又十方世界所有眾聲，上中下音，皆能變之，令作佛聲，演出無常、苦、空、無我之音。及十方諸佛所說種種之法，皆於其中普令得聞。舍利弗！我今略說菩薩不可思議解脫之力，若廣說者，窮劫不盡。」

6.066 是時，大迦葉聞說菩薩不可思議解脫法門，歎未曾有，謂舍利弗：「譬如有人，於盲者前現眾色像，非彼所見；一切聲聞，聞是不可思議解脫法門，不能解了，為若此也！智者聞是，其誰不發阿耨多羅三藐三菩提心？我等何為永絕其根，於此大乘，已如敗種！一切聲聞，聞是不可思議解脫法門，皆應號泣，聲震三千大千世界；一切菩薩，應大欣慶，頂受此法。若有菩薩信解不可思議解脫法門者，一切魔眾無如之何。」大迦葉說是語時，三萬二千天子，皆發阿耨多羅三藐三菩提心。

6.067 爾時，維摩詰語大迦葉：「仁者！十方無量阿僧祇世界中作魔王者，多是住不可思議解脫菩薩。以方便力故，教化眾生，現作魔王。又迦葉！十方無量菩薩，或有人從乞手足耳鼻、頭目髓腦、血肉皮骨、聚落城邑、妻子奴婢、象馬車乘、金銀琉璃、硨磲、碼碯、珊瑚、琥珀、真珠珂貝、衣服飲食，如此乞者，多是住不可思議解脫菩薩，以方便力，而往試之，令其堅固。所以者何？住不可思議解脫菩薩，有威德力故，現行逼迫，示諸眾生，如是難事；凡夫下劣，無有力勢，不能如是逼迫菩薩。譬如龍象蹴踏，非驢所堪，是名住不可思議解脫菩薩智慧方便之門。」

觀眾生品第七

爾時，文殊師利問維摩詰言：「菩薩云何觀於眾生?」

維摩詰言：「譬如幻師，見所幻人，菩薩觀眾生為若此。如智者見水中月，如鏡中見其面像，如熱時焰，如呼聲響，如空中雲，如水聚沫，如水上泡，如芭蕉堅，如電久住，如第五大，如第六陰，如第七情，如十三入，如十九界，菩薩觀眾生為若此。如無色界色，如焦穀芽，如須陀洹身見，如阿那含入胎，如阿羅漢三毒，如得忍菩薩貪恚毀禁，如佛煩惱習，如盲者見色，如入滅盡定出入息，如空中鳥跡，如石女兒，如化人起煩惱，如夢所見已寤，如滅度者受身，如無煙之火，菩薩觀眾生為若此。」

文殊師利言：「若菩薩作是觀者，云何行慈? 」 7.068

維摩詰言：「菩薩作是觀已，自念：『我當為眾生說如斯法。』是即真實慈也。

行寂滅慈，無所生故；行不熱慈，無煩惱故；

行等之慈，等三世故；行無諍慈，無所起故；
行不二慈，內外不合故；行不壞慈，畢竟盡故；
行堅固慈，心無毀故；行清淨慈，諸法性淨故；
行無邊慈，如虛空故；行阿羅漢慈，破結賊故；
7.069 行菩薩慈，安眾生故；行如來慈，得如相故；
行佛之慈，覺眾生故；行自然慈，無因得故；
行菩提慈，等一味故；行無等慈，斷諸愛故；
行大悲慈，導以大乘故；行無厭慈，觀空無我故；
7.070 行法施慈，無遺惜故；行持戒慈，化毀禁故；
行忍辱慈，護彼我故；行精進慈，荷負眾生故；
行禪定慈，不受味故；行智慧慈，無不知時故；
行方便慈，一切示現故；行無隱慈，直心清淨故；
行深心慈，無雜行故；行無誑慈，不虛假故；
行安樂慈，令得佛樂故。菩薩之慈，為若此也。」

7.071 文殊師利又問：「何謂為悲？」

答曰：「菩薩所作功德，皆與一切眾生共之。」

「何謂為喜？」

答曰：「有所饒益，歡喜無悔。」

「何謂為捨？」

答曰：「所作福祐，無所悕望。」

文殊師利又問：「生死有畏，菩薩當何所依？」

維摩詰言：「菩薩於生死畏中，當依如來功德之力。」

文殊師利又問：「菩薩欲依如來功德之力，當於何住？」

答曰：「菩薩欲依如來功德力者，當住度脫一切眾生。」

又問：「欲度眾生，當何所除？」 7.072

答曰：「欲度眾生，除其煩惱。」

又問：「欲除煩惱，當何所行？」

答曰：「當行正念。」

又問：「云何行於正念？」

答曰：「當行不生不滅。」

又問：「何法不生？何法不滅？」

答曰：「不善不生，善法不滅。」

又問：「善不善孰為本？」

答曰：「身為本。」 7.073

又問：「身孰為本？」

答曰：「欲貪為本。」

又問：「欲貪孰為本？」

答曰：「虛妄分別為本。」

又問：「虛妄分別孰為本？」

答曰：「顛倒想為本。」

又問：「顛倒想孰為本？」

答曰：「無住為本。」

又問：「無住孰為本？」

答曰：「無住則無本。文殊師利！從無住本，立一切法。」

時維摩詰室有一天女，見諸大人，聞所說法，便現其身，即以天華，散諸菩薩、大弟子上。華至諸菩薩，即皆墮落，至大弟子，便著不墮。一切弟子神力去華，不能令去。

7.074 爾時天問舍利弗：「何故去華？」

答曰：「此華不如法，是以去之。」

天曰：「勿謂此華為不如法。所以者何？是華無所分別，仁者自生分別想耳！若於佛法出家，有所分別，為不如法；若無所分別，是則如法。觀諸菩薩華不著者，已斷一切分別想故。譬如人畏時，非人得其便；如是弟子畏生死故，色、聲、香、味、觸得其便也。已離畏者，一切五欲無能為也；結習未盡，華著身耳！結習盡者，華不著也。」

舍利弗言：「天止此室，其已久如？」

7.075 答曰：「我止此室，如耆年解脫。」

舍利弗言：「止此久耶？」

天曰：「耆年解脫，亦何如久？」

舍利弗默然不答。天曰：「如何耆舊，大智而默？」

答曰：「解脫者無所言說，故吾於是不知所云。」

天曰：「言說文字，皆解脫相。所以者何？解脫者，不內、不外，不在兩間，文字亦不內不外，不在兩間。是故，舍利弗！無離文字說解脫也。所以者何？一切諸法是解脫相。」

舍利弗言：「不復以離婬、怒、癡為解脫乎？」

天曰：「佛為增上慢人，說離婬、怒、癡為解脫耳；若無增上慢者，佛說婬、怒、癡性，即是解脫。」

舍利弗言：「善哉，善哉！天女！汝何所得？以何為證？辯乃如是！」

天曰：「我無得無證，故辯如是。所以者何？若有 7.076
得有證者，即於佛法為增上慢。」

舍利弗問天：「汝於三乘，為何志求？」

天曰：「以聲聞法化眾生故，我為聲聞；以因緣法化眾生故，我為辟支佛；以大悲法化眾生故，我為大乘。舍利弗！如人入瞻蔔林，唯嗅瞻蔔，不嗅餘香。如是，若入此室，但聞佛功德之香，不樂聞聲聞、辟支佛功德香也。舍利弗！其有釋、梵、四天王，諸天、龍、鬼神等，入此室者，聞斯上人講說正法，皆樂佛功德之香，發心而出。舍利弗！吾止此室，十有二年，初不聞說聲聞、辟支佛法，但聞菩薩大慈大悲，不可思議諸佛之法。

「舍利弗！此室常現八未曾有難得之法。何等為八？ 7.077

此室常以金色光照，晝夜無異，不以日月所照為明，是為一未曾有難得之法；
此室入者，不為諸垢之所惱也，是為二未曾有難得之法；
此室常有釋梵四天王、他方菩薩來會不絕，是為三未曾有難得之法；

此室常說六波羅蜜不退轉法，是為四未曾有難得之法；
此室常作天人第一之樂，絃出無量法化之聲，是為五未曾有難得之法；
此室有四大藏，眾寶積滿，賙窮濟乏，求得無盡，是為六未曾有難得之法；
7.078 此室釋迦牟尼佛、阿彌陀佛、阿閦佛、寶德、寶炎、寶月、寶嚴、難勝、師子響、一切利成，如是等十方無量諸佛，是上人念時，即皆為來，廣說諸佛秘要法藏，說已還去，是為七未曾有難得之法；
此室一切諸天嚴飾宮殿，諸佛淨土，皆於中現，是為八未曾有難得之法。

「舍利弗！此室常現八未曾有難得之法，誰有見斯不思議事，而復樂於聲聞法乎？」

舍利弗言：「汝何以不轉女身？」

天曰：「我從十二年來，求女人相了不可得。當何所轉？譬如幻師化作幻女，若有人問：『何以不轉女身？』是人為正問不？」

舍利弗言：「不也！幻無定相，當何所轉？」

7.079 天曰：「一切諸法亦復如是，無有定相，云何乃問不轉女身？」

即時天女以神通力，變舍利弗令如天女，天自化身如舍利弗，而問言：「何以不轉女身？」

舍利弗以天女像而答言：「我今不知何轉而變為女身？」

天曰：「舍利弗！若能轉此女身，則一切女人亦當能轉。如舍利弗非女而現女身，一切女人亦復如是，雖現女身，而非女也。是故佛說一切諸法非男、非女。」

即時天女還攝神力，舍利弗身還復如故。天問舍利弗：「女身色相，今何所在？」

舍利弗言：「女身色相，無在無不在。」

天曰：「一切諸法，亦復如是，無在無不在。夫無在無不在者，佛所說也。」

舍利弗問天：「汝於此沒，當生何所？」

天曰：「佛化所生，吾如彼生。」

曰：「佛化所生，非沒生也。」

天曰：「眾生猶然，無沒生也。」

舍利弗問天：「汝久如當得阿耨多羅三藐三菩提？」 7.080

天曰：「如舍利弗還為凡夫，我乃當成阿耨多羅三藐三菩提。」

舍利弗言：「我作凡夫，無有是處。」

天曰：「我得阿耨多羅三藐三菩提，亦無是處。所以者何？菩提無住處，是故無有得者。」

舍利弗言：「今諸佛得阿耨多羅三藐三菩提，已得當得，如恒河沙，皆謂何乎？」

天曰：「皆以世俗文字數故，說有三世，非謂菩提有去來今。」

天曰:「舍利弗!汝得阿羅漢道耶?」

曰:「無所得故而得。」

天曰:「諸佛、菩薩亦復如是,無所得故而得。」

爾時,維摩詰語舍利弗:「是天女已曾供養九十二億佛,已能遊戲菩薩神通,所願具足,得無生忍,住不退轉;以本願故,隨意能現,教化眾生。」

佛道品第八

爾時，文殊師利問維摩詰言：「菩薩云何通達佛道？」

維摩詰言：「若菩薩行於非道，是為通達佛道。」

又問：「云何菩薩行於非道？」

答曰：「若菩薩行五無間，而無惱恚；

至于地獄，無諸罪垢；
至于畜生，無有無明憍慢等過；
至于餓鬼，而具足功德；
行色、無色界道，不以為勝。
示行貪欲，離諸染著； 8.081
示行瞋恚，於諸眾生，無有恚閡；
示行愚癡，而以智慧，調伏其心。
示行慳貪，而捨內外所有，不惜身命；
示行毀禁，而安住淨戒，乃至小罪，猶懷大懼；
示行瞋恚，而常慈忍；
示行懈怠，而懃修功德；

示行亂意，而常念定；
示行愚癡，而通達世間、出世間慧；
示行諂偽，而善方便，隨諸經義；
示行憍慢，而於眾生，猶如橋梁；
示行諸煩惱，而心常清淨；
示入於魔，而順佛智慧，不隨他教；
示入聲聞，而為眾生，說未聞法；
8.082 示入辟支佛，而成就大悲，教化眾生；
示入貧窮，而有寶手，功德無盡；
示入刑殘，而具諸相好，以自莊嚴；
示入下賤，而生佛種姓中，具諸功德；
示入羸劣醜陋，而得那羅延身，一切眾生之所樂見；
示入老病，而永斷病根，超越死畏；
8.083 示有資生，而恒觀無常，實無所貪；
示有妻妾采女，而常遠離五欲淤泥；
現於訥鈍，而成就辯才，總持無失；
示入邪濟，而以正濟，度諸眾生；
現遍入諸道，而斷其因緣；
現於涅槃，而不斷生死。

「文殊師利！菩薩能如是行於非道，是為通達佛道。」

於是維摩詰問文殊師利：「何等為如來種？」

8.084 文殊師利言：「有身為種，無明有愛為種，貪恚癡為種，四顛倒為種，五蓋為種，六入為種，七識處為種，八邪法為種，九惱處為種，十不善道為種。以要言之，六十二見及一切煩惱，皆是佛種。」

曰：「何謂也？」

答曰：「若見無為入正位者，不能復發阿耨多羅三藐三菩提心；譬如高原陸地，不生蓮華，卑濕淤泥，乃生此華；如是見無為法入正位者，終不復能生於佛法；煩惱泥中，乃有眾生起佛法耳！又如植種於 8.085
空，終不得生！糞壤之地，乃能滋茂。如是入無為正位者，不生佛法；起於我見如須彌山，猶能發于阿耨多羅三藐三菩提心，生佛法矣！是故當知，一切煩惱，為如來種。譬如不下巨海，不能得無價寶珠。如是不入煩惱大海，則不能得一切智寶。」

爾時，大迦葉歎言：「善哉，善哉！文殊師利！快說此語。誠如所言，塵勞之疇為如來種；我等今者，不復堪任發阿耨多羅三藐三菩提心，乃至五無間罪，猶能發意生於佛法，而今我等永不能發。譬如根敗之士，其於五欲不能復利。如是聲聞諸結斷者，於佛法中無所復益，永不志願。是故，文殊師利！凡夫於佛法有反復，而聲聞無也。所以者何？凡夫聞佛法，能起無上道心，不斷三寶。正使聲聞終身聞佛法，力、無畏等，永不能發無上道意。」

爾時，會中有菩薩，名普現色身，問維摩詰言： 8.086
「居士！父母妻子、親戚眷屬、吏民知識，悉為是誰？奴婢僮僕、象馬車乘，皆何所在？」

於是維摩詰以偈答曰：

「智度菩薩母，方便以為父，
一切眾導師，無不由是生。
法喜以為妻，慈悲心為女，
善心誠實男，畢竟空寂舍。
弟子眾塵勞，隨意之所轉，
道品善知識，由是成正覺。

8.087 諸度法等侶，四攝為伎女，
歌詠誦法言，以此為音樂。
總持之園苑，無漏法林樹，
覺意淨妙華，解脫智慧果。
八解之浴池，定水湛然滿，
布以七淨華，浴此無垢人。
象馬五通馳，大乘以為車，
調御以一心，遊於八正路。
相具以嚴容，眾好飾其姿，
慚愧之上服，深心為華鬘。
富有七財寶，教授以滋息，
如所說修行，迴向為大利。
四禪為床座，從於淨命生，
多聞增智慧，以為自覺音。
8.088 甘露法之食，解脫味為漿，
淨心以澡浴，戒品為塗香。
摧滅煩惱賊，勇健無能踰，
降伏四種魔，勝幡建道場。
雖知無起滅，示彼故有生，
悉現諸國土，如日無不見。
供養於十方，無量億如來，
諸佛及己身，無有分別想。
雖知諸佛國，及與眾生空，
而常修淨土，教化於群生。
諸有眾生類，形聲及威儀，
無畏力菩薩，一時能盡現。
覺知眾魔事，而示隨其行，
以善方便智，隨意皆能現。
8.089 或示老病死，成就諸群生，
了知如幻化，通達無有礙。

或現劫盡燒，天地皆洞然，
眾人有常想，照令知無常。
無數億眾生，俱來請菩薩，
一時到其舍，化令向佛道。
經書禁呪術，工巧諸伎藝，
盡現行此事，饒益諸群生。
世間眾道法，悉於中出家，
因以解人惑，而不墮邪見。
或作日月天，梵王世界主，
或時作地水，或復作風火。
劫中有疾疫，現作諸藥草， 8.090
若有服之者，除病消眾毒。
劫中有飢饉，現身作飲食，
先救彼飢渴，却以法語人。
劫中有刀兵，為之起慈心，
化彼諸眾生，令住無諍地。
若有大戰陣，立之以等力，
菩薩現威勢，降伏使和安。
一切國土中，諸有地獄處，
輒往到于彼，勉濟其苦惱。
一切國土中，畜生相食噉，
皆現生於彼，為之作利益。
示受於五欲，亦復現行禪，
令魔心憒亂，不能得其便。
火中生蓮華，是可謂希有， 8.091
在欲而行禪，希有亦如是。
或現作婬女，引諸好色者，
先以欲鉤牽，後令入佛道。
或為邑中主，或作商人導，
國師及大臣，以祐利眾生。

諸有貧窮者，現作無盡藏，
因以勸導之，令發菩提心。
我心憍慢者，為現大力士，
消伏諸貢高，令住無上道。
其有恐懼眾，居前而慰安，
先施以無畏，後令發道心。
或現離婬欲，為五通仙人，
開導諸群生，令住戒忍慈。
8.092 見須供事者，現為作僮僕，
既悅可其意，乃發以道心。
隨彼之所須，得入於佛道，
以善方便力，皆能給足之。
如是道無量，所行無有涯，
智慧無邊際，度脫無數眾。
假令一切佛，於無量億劫，
讚歎其功德，猶尚不能盡。
誰聞如是法，不發菩提心，
除彼不肖人，癡冥無智者。」

入不二法門品第九

爾時，維摩詰謂眾菩薩言：「諸仁者！云何菩薩入不二法門？各隨所樂說之。」

會中有菩薩名法自在，說言：「諸仁者！生滅為二。法本不生，今則無滅，得此無生法忍，是為入不二法門。」

德守菩薩曰：「我、我所為二。因有我故，便有我所；若無有我，則無我所，是為入不二法門。」

不眴菩薩曰：「受、不受為二。若法不受，則不可 9.093
得；以不可得，故無取無捨、無作無行，是為入不二法門。」

德頂菩薩曰：「垢、淨為二。見垢實性，則無淨相，順於滅相，是為入不二法門。」

善宿菩薩曰：「是動、是念為二。不動則無念，無念則無分別。通達此者，是為入不二法門。」

善眼菩薩曰：「一相、無相為二。若知一相即是無相，亦不取無相，入於平等，是為入不二法門。」

妙臂菩薩曰：「菩薩心、聲聞心為二。觀心相空，如幻化者，無菩薩心、無聲聞心，是為入不二法門。」

9.094 弗沙菩薩曰：「善、不善為二。若不起善、不善，入無相際而通達者，是為入不二法門。」

師子菩薩曰：「罪、福為二。若達罪性，則與福無異，以金剛慧決了此相，無縛無解者，是為入不二法門。」

師子意菩薩曰：「有漏、無漏為二。若得諸法等，則不起漏、不漏想，不著於相，亦不住無相，是為入不二法門。」

淨解菩薩曰：「有為、無為為二。若離一切數，則心如虛空，以清淨慧無所礙者，是為入不二法門。」

那羅延菩薩曰：「世間、出世間為二。世間性空，即是出世間。於其中不入、不出、不溢、不散，是為入不二法門。」

9.095 善意菩薩曰：「生死、涅槃為二。若見生死性，則無生死，無縛無解，不生不滅，如是解者，是為入不二法門。」

現見菩薩曰：「盡、不盡為二。法若究竟，盡若不盡，皆是無盡相；無盡相即是空，空則無有盡不盡相。如是入者，是為入不二法門。」

普守菩薩曰：「我、無我為二。我尚不可得，非我何可得？見我實性者，不復起二，是為入不二法門。」

電天菩薩曰：「明、無明為二。無明實性即是明，明亦不可取，離一切數，於其中平等無二者，是為入不二法門。」

喜見菩薩曰：「色、色空為二。色即是空，非色滅空，色性自空。如是受、想、行、識、識空為二，識即是空，非識滅空，識性自空，於其中而通達者，是為入不二法門。」

明相菩薩曰：「四種異、空種異為二。四種性即是 9.096
空種性，如前際、後際空，故中際亦空。若能如是知諸種性者，是為入不二法門。」

妙意菩薩曰：「眼、色為二。若知眼性，於色不貪、不恚、不癡，是名寂滅。如是耳聲、鼻香、舌味、身觸、意法為二，若知意性，於法不貪、不恚、不癡，是名寂滅，安住其中，是為入不二法門。」

無盡意菩薩曰：「布施、迴向一切智為二。布施性即是迴向一切智性，如是持戒、忍辱、精進、禪定、智慧、迴向一切智為二，智慧性即是迴向一切智性，於其中入一相者，是為入不二法門。」

深慧菩薩曰：「是空、是無相、是無作為二。空即無相，無相即無作；若空、無相、無作，則無心意識。於一解脫門即是三解脫門者，是為入不二法門。」

寂根菩薩曰：「佛、法、眾為二。佛即是法，法即 9.097
是眾，是三寶皆無為相，與虛空等，一切法亦爾。能隨此行者，是為入不二法門。」

心無礙菩薩曰：「身、身滅為二。身即是身滅。所以者何？見身實相者，不起見身及見滅身，身與滅身無二無分別，於其中不驚、不懼者，是為入不二法門。」

上善菩薩曰：「身、口、意善為二。是三業皆無作相，身無作相，即口無作相；口無作相，即意無作相；是三業無作相，即一切法無作相。能如是隨無作慧者，是為入不二法門。」

福田菩薩曰：「福行、罪行、不動行為二。三行實性即是空，空則無福行、無罪行、無不動行。於此三行而不起者，是為入不二法門。」

9.098 華嚴菩薩曰：「從我起二為二。見我實相者，不起二法；若不住二法，則無有識。無所識者，是為入不二法門。」

德藏菩薩曰：「有所得相為二。若無所得，則無取捨。無取捨者，是為入不二法門。」

月上菩薩曰：「闇與明為二。無闇、無明，則無有二。所以者何？如入滅受想定，無闇、無明，一切法相亦復如是，於其中平等入者，是為入不二法門。」

寶印手菩薩曰：「樂涅槃、不樂世間為二。若不樂涅槃、不厭世間，則無有二。所以者何？若有縛，則有解。若本無縛，其誰求解？無縛無解，則無樂厭，是為入不二法門。」

珠頂王菩薩曰：「正道、邪道為二。住正道者，則不分別是邪是正，離此二者，是為入不二法門。」

樂實菩薩曰：「實、不實為二。實見者尚不見實，何況非實！所以者何？非肉眼所見，慧眼乃能見，而此慧眼，無見無不見，是為入不二法門。」

如是諸菩薩各各說已，問文殊師利：「何等是菩薩入不二法門？」

文殊師利曰：「如我意者，於一切法無言無說，無示無識，離諸問答，是為入不二法門。」

於是文殊師利問維摩詰：「我等各自說已，仁者當說，何等是菩薩入不二法門？」

時維摩詰默然無言。 9.099

文殊師利歎曰：「善哉！善哉！乃至無有文字、語言，是真入不二法門。」

說是入不二法門品時，於此眾中，五千菩薩皆入不二法門，得無生法忍。

香積佛品第十

於是舍利弗心念：「日時欲至，此諸菩薩當於何食？」

時維摩詰知其意而語言：「佛說八解脫，仁者受行，豈雜欲食而聞法乎？若欲食者，且待須臾，當令汝得未曾有食。」

時維摩詰即入三昧，以神通力示諸大眾，上方界分過四十二恒河沙佛土，有國名眾香，佛號香積，今現在，其國香氣，比於十方諸佛世界人、天之香，最為第一。彼土無有聲聞、辟支佛名，唯有清淨大菩薩眾，佛為說法。其界一切，皆以香作樓閣，經行香地，苑園皆香，其食香氣，周流十方無量世界。時彼佛與諸菩薩方共坐食，有諸天子皆號香嚴，悉發阿耨多羅三藐三菩提心，供養彼佛及諸菩薩，此諸大眾莫不目見。

時維摩詰問眾菩薩言：「諸仁者！誰能致彼佛飯？」 10.100
以文殊師利威神力故，咸皆默然。維摩詰言：「仁此大眾，無乃可恥？」

文殊師利曰：「如佛所言，勿輕未學。」

於是維摩詰不起于座，居眾會前，化作菩薩，相好光明，威德殊勝，蔽於眾會，而告之曰：「汝往上方界分，度如四十二恒河沙佛土，有國名眾香，佛號香積，與諸菩薩方共坐食。汝往到彼，如我辭曰：『維摩詰稽首世尊足下！致敬無量，問訊起居，少病少惱，氣力安不？願得世尊所食之餘，當於娑婆世界施作佛事，令此樂小法者得弘大道，亦使如來名聲普聞。』」

10.101 時化菩薩即於會前，昇于上方，舉眾皆見其去，到眾香界，禮彼佛足，又聞其言：「維摩詰稽首世尊足下！致敬無量，問訊起居，少病少惱，氣力安不？願得世尊所食之餘，欲於娑婆世界施作佛事，使此樂小法者得弘大道，亦使如來名聲普聞。」

彼諸大士見化菩薩，歎未曾有：「今此上人從何所來？娑婆世界為在何許？云何名為樂小法者？」即以問佛。佛告之曰：「下方度如四十二恒河沙佛土，有世界名娑婆，佛號釋迦牟尼，今現在。於五濁惡世，為樂小法眾生敷演道教；彼有菩薩名維摩詰，住不可思議解脫，為諸菩薩說法，故遣化來，稱揚我名，并讚此土，令彼菩薩增益功德。」

10.102 彼菩薩言：「其人何如，乃作是化？德力無畏，神足若斯！」佛言：「甚大！一切十方皆遣化往，施作佛事，饒益眾生。」

於是香積如來以眾香鉢，盛滿香飯，與化菩薩。時彼九百萬菩薩俱發聲言：「我欲詣娑婆世界供養釋迦牟尼佛，并欲見維摩詰等諸菩薩眾。」

佛言：「可往。攝汝身香，無令彼諸眾生起惑著心。又當捨汝本形，勿使彼國求菩薩者，而自鄙恥。又汝於彼莫懷輕賤，而作礙想。所以者何？十方國土，皆如虛空。又諸佛為欲化諸樂小法者，不盡現其清淨土耳！」時化菩薩既受鉢飯，與彼九百萬菩薩俱，承佛威神，及維摩詰力，於彼世界，忽然不現，須臾之間，至維摩詰舍。

時維摩詰即化作九百萬師子之座，嚴好如前，諸菩 10.103
薩皆坐其上。是化菩薩以滿鉢香飯與維摩詰，飯香普熏毘耶離城，及三千大千世界。時毘耶離婆羅門、居士等，聞是香氣，身意快然，歎未曾有！於是長者主月蓋從八萬四千人，來入維摩詰舍。見其室中菩薩甚多，諸師子座，高廣嚴好，皆大歡喜，禮眾菩薩及大弟子，却住一面。諸地神、虛空神及欲、色界諸天，聞此香氣，亦皆來入維摩詰舍。

時維摩詰語舍利弗等諸大聲聞：「仁者可食，如來 10.104
甘露味飯，大悲所熏，無以限意食之，使不消也。」有異聲聞念：「是飯少，而此大眾人人當食？」化菩薩曰：「勿以聲聞小德小智，稱量如來無量福慧！四海有竭，此飯無盡！使一切人食，揣若須彌，乃至一劫，猶不能盡。所以者何？無盡戒、定、智慧、解脫、解脫知見功德具足者，所食之餘，終不可盡。」於是鉢飯悉飽眾會，猶故不𣩵。其諸菩薩、聲聞、天、人，食此飯者，身安快樂，譬如一切樂莊嚴國諸菩薩也；又諸毛孔皆出妙香，亦如眾香國土諸樹之香。

爾時，維摩詰問眾香菩薩：「香積如來以何說法？」 10.105

彼菩薩曰：「我土如來無文字說，但以眾香令諸天、人得入律行。菩薩各各坐香樹下，聞斯妙香，即獲一切德藏三昧。得是三昧者，菩薩所有功德皆悉具足。」

彼諸菩薩問維摩詰：「今世尊釋迦牟尼以何說法？」

維摩詰言：「此土眾生剛強難化，故佛為說剛強之語以調伏之。

言是地獄、是畜生、是餓鬼，是諸難處，是愚人生處；
是身邪行，是身邪行報；是口邪行，是口邪行報；是意邪行，是意邪行報；
是殺生，是殺生報；是不與取，是不與取報；是邪婬，是邪婬報；是妄語，是妄語報；是兩舌，是兩舌報；是惡口，是惡口報；是無義語，是無義語報；
10.106 是貪嫉，是貪嫉報；是瞋惱，是瞋惱報；
是邪見，是邪見報；是慳悋，是慳悋報；
是毀戒，是毀戒報；是瞋恚，是瞋恚報；
是懈怠，是懈怠報；是亂意，是亂意報；
是愚癡，是愚癡報；是結戒，是持戒，是犯戒；
是應作，是不應作；是障礙，是不障礙；
10.107 是得罪，是離罪；是淨，是垢；
是有漏，是無漏；是邪道，是正道；
是有為，是無為；是世間，是涅槃。

「以難化之人，心如猨猴，故以若干種法，制御其心，乃可調伏。譬如象馬，𢤱悷不調，加諸楚毒，乃至徹骨，然後調伏。如是剛強難化眾生，故以一切苦切之言，乃可入律。」

彼諸菩薩聞說是已，皆曰：「未曾有也！如世尊釋迦牟尼佛，隱其無量自在之力，乃以貧所樂法，度脫眾生；斯諸菩薩亦能勞謙，以無量大悲，生是佛土。」

維摩詰言：「此土菩薩於諸眾生大悲堅固，誠如所言。然其一世饒益眾生，多於彼國百千劫行。所以者何？此娑婆世界有十事善法，諸餘淨土之所無有。何等為十？以布施攝貧窮，以淨戒攝毀禁，以忍辱攝瞋恚，以精進攝懈怠，以禪定攝亂意，以智慧攝愚癡，說除難法度八難者，以大乘法度樂小乘者，以諸善根濟無德者，常以四攝成就眾生，是為十。」 10.108

彼菩薩曰：「菩薩成就幾法？於此世界行無瘡疣，生于淨土。」 10.109

維摩詰言：「菩薩成就八法，於此世界行無瘡疣，生于淨土。何等為八？饒益眾生，而不望報；代一切眾生受諸苦惱，所作功德盡以施之；等心眾生，謙下無礙；於諸菩薩視之如佛；所未聞經，聞之不疑；不與聲聞而相違背；不嫉彼供，不高己利，而於其中調伏其心；常省己過，不訟彼短，恒以一心求諸功德，是為八法。」

維摩詰、文殊師利於大眾中說是法時，百千天、人皆發阿耨多羅三藐三菩提心，十千菩薩得無生法忍。

菩薩行品第十一

是時佛說法於菴羅樹園，其地忽然廣博嚴事，一切眾會皆作金色。阿難白佛言：「世尊！以何因緣，有此瑞應？是處忽然廣博嚴事，一切眾會皆作金色。」

佛告阿難：「是維摩詰、文殊師利，與諸大眾恭敬圍繞，發意欲來，故先為此瑞應。」

於是維摩詰語文殊師利：「可共見佛，與諸菩薩禮事供養。」

文殊師利言：「善哉！行矣！今正是時。」 11.110

維摩詰即以神力，持諸大眾并師子座，置於右掌，往詣佛所。到已著地，稽首佛足，右遶七匝，一心合掌，在一面立；其諸菩薩即皆避座，稽首佛足，亦繞七匝，於一面立；諸大弟子、釋、梵、四天王等，亦皆避座，稽首佛足，在一面立。

於是世尊如法慰問諸菩薩已，各令復坐，即皆受教。眾坐已定，佛語舍利弗：「汝見菩薩大士，自在神力之所為乎？」

11.111 「唯然，已見！」

「於汝意云何？」「世尊！我覩其為不可思議，非意所圖，非度所測。」

爾時，阿難白佛言：「世尊！今所聞香，自昔未有，是為何香？」

佛告阿難：「是彼菩薩毛孔之香。」

於是舍利弗語阿難言：「我等毛孔亦出是香。」

阿難言：「此所從來？」

曰：「是長者維摩詰，從眾香國，取佛餘飯，於舍食者，一切毛孔皆香若此。」

阿難問維摩詰：「是香氣住當久如？」

維摩詰言：「至此飯消。」

11.112 曰：「此飯久如當消？」

曰：「此飯勢力至于七日，然後乃消。又阿難！若聲聞人未入正位，食此飯者，得入正位，然後乃消；已入正位，食此飯者，得心解脫，然後乃消；若未發大乘意，食此飯者，至發意乃消；已發意食此飯者，得無生忍，然後乃消；已得無生忍，食此飯者，至一生補處，然後乃消。譬如有藥，名曰上味，其有服者，身諸毒滅，然後乃消。此飯如是，滅除一切諸煩惱毒，然後乃消。」

阿難白佛言：「未曾有也，世尊！如此香飯能作佛事。」

佛言:「如是,如是!阿難!或有佛土以佛光明而作佛事,有以諸菩薩而作佛事,有以佛所化人而作佛事,有以菩提樹而作佛事,有以佛衣服、臥具而作佛事,有以飯食而作佛事,有以園林臺觀而作佛事,有以三十二相、八十隨形好而作佛事,有以佛身而作佛事,有以虛空而作佛事;眾生應以此緣得入律行。有以夢、幻、影、響、鏡中像、水中月、熱時燄,如是等喻而作佛事。有以音聲、語言、文字而作佛事。或有清淨佛土、寂寞無言、無說、無示、無識、無作、無為,而作佛事。如是,阿難!諸佛威儀進止,諸所施為,無非佛事。 11.113

「阿難!有此四魔,八萬四千諸煩惱門,而諸眾生為之疲勞,諸佛即以此法而作佛事,是名入一切諸佛法門。菩薩入此門者,若見一切淨好佛土,不以為喜,不貪不高;若見一切不淨佛土,不以為憂,不礙不沒;但於諸佛生清淨心,歡喜恭敬,未曾有也!諸佛如來功德平等!為化眾生故,而現佛土不同。阿難!汝見諸佛國土,地有若干,而虛空無若干也;如是見諸佛色身有若干耳,其無礙慧無若干也。 11.114

「阿難!諸佛色身、威相、種性,戒、定、智慧、解脫、解脫知見,力、無所畏、不共之法、大慈、大悲,威儀所行,及其壽命,說法教化,成就眾生,淨佛國土,具諸佛法,悉皆同等,是故名為三藐三佛陀,名為多陀阿伽度,名為佛陀。阿難!若我廣說此三句義,汝以劫壽,不能盡受;正使三千大千世界滿中眾生,皆如阿難多聞第一,得念總持,此諸人等,以劫之壽,亦不能受。如是,阿難!諸佛阿耨多羅三藐三菩提,無有限量,智慧辯才不可思議。」

阿難白佛言：「我從今已往，不敢自謂以為多聞。」

11.115 佛告阿難：「勿起退意！所以者何？我說汝於聲聞中為最多聞，非謂菩薩。且止，阿難！其有智者不應限度諸菩薩也；一切海淵尚可測量，菩薩禪定、智慧、總持、辯才一切功德不可量也。阿難！汝等捨置菩薩所行，是維摩詰一時所現神通之力、一切聲聞、辟支佛於百千劫，盡力變化所不能作。」

爾時，眾香世界菩薩來者，合掌白佛言：「世尊！我等初見此土，生下劣想，今自悔責，捨離是心。所以者何？諸佛方便，不可思議！為度眾生故，隨其所應，現佛國異。唯然世尊！願賜少法，還於彼土，當念如來。」

佛告諸菩薩：「有盡無盡解脫法門，汝等當學。何謂為盡？謂有為法；何謂無盡？謂無為法。如菩薩者，不盡有為，不住無為。

11.116 「何謂不盡有為？謂不離大慈，不捨大悲；深發一切智心，而不忽忘；教化眾生，終不厭倦；於四攝法，常念順行；護持正法，不惜軀命；種諸善根，無有疲厭。志常安住，方便迴向；求法不懈，說法
11.117 無悋；勤供諸佛。故入生死而無所畏；於諸榮辱，心無憂喜；不輕未學，敬學如佛；墮煩惱者，令發正念，於遠離樂，不以為貴；不著己樂，慶於彼樂。在諸禪定，如地獄想；於生死中，如園觀想；見來求者，為善師想；捨諸所有，具一切智想；見毀戒人，起救護想；諸波羅蜜，為父母想；道品之法，為眷屬想。發行善根，無有齊限；以諸淨國嚴
11.118 飾之事，成己佛土；行無限施，具足相好；除一切惡，淨身口意。生死無數劫，意而有勇；聞佛無量

德，志而不倦。以智慧劍，破煩惱賊；出陰界入，
荷負眾生，永使解脫。以大精進，摧伏魔軍，常求
無念實相智慧行；於世間法少欲知足，於出世間求 11.119
之無厭，而不捨世間法，不壞威儀法而能隨俗。起
神通慧，引導眾生，得念總持，所聞不忘。善別諸
根，斷眾生疑；以樂說辯，演法無礙。淨十善道，
受天、人福；修四無量，開梵天道。勸請說法，隨
喜讚善，得佛音聲；身口意善，得佛威儀。深修善
法，所行轉勝；以大乘教，成菩薩僧；心無放逸，
不失眾善。行如此法，是名菩薩不盡有為。

「何謂菩薩不住無為？謂修學空，不以空為證；修學 11.120
無相、無作，不以無相、無作為證；修學無起，不以
無起為證。觀於無常，而不厭善本；觀世間苦，而不
惡生死；觀於無我，而誨人不倦；觀於寂滅，而不
永滅；觀於遠離，而身心修善；觀無所歸，而歸趣
善法；觀於無生，而以生法荷負一切；觀於無漏， 11.121
而不斷諸漏；觀無所行，而以行法教化眾生；觀於
空無，而不捨大悲；觀正法位，而不隨小乘；觀諸
法虛妄，無牢無人、無主無相，本願未滿，而不虛
福德、禪定、智慧。修如此法，是名菩薩不住無為。

「又具福德故，不住無為；具智慧故，不盡有為。
大慈悲故，不住無為；滿本願故，不盡有為。集法 11.122
藥故，不住無為；隨授藥故，不盡有為。知眾生病
故，不住無為；滅眾生病故，不盡有為。諸正士菩
薩以修此法，不盡有為、不住無為，是名盡無盡解
脫法門，汝等當學！」

爾時，彼諸菩薩聞說是法，皆大歡喜，以眾妙華、
若干種色、若干種香，散遍三千大千世界，供養於

佛，及此經法，并諸菩薩已，稽首佛足，歎未曾有！言：「釋迦牟尼佛乃能於此善行方便。」言已，忽然不現，還到彼國。

見阿閦佛品第十二

爾時，世尊問維摩詰：「汝欲見如來，為以何等觀如來乎？」

維摩詰言：「如自觀身實相，觀佛亦然。我觀如來
前際不來，後際不去，今則不住。不觀色，不觀色
如，不觀色性。不觀受、想、行、識，不觀識如，
不觀識性，非四大起，同於虛空。六入無積，眼、 12.123
耳、鼻、舌、身、心已過；不在三界，三垢已離。順
三脫門，具足三明，與無明等。不一相、不異相，不
自相、不他相，非無相、非取相。不此岸，不彼岸，
不中流，而化眾生。觀於寂滅，亦不永滅。不此不 12.124
彼；不以此，不以彼。不可以智知，不可以識識。
無晦無明，無名無相，無強無弱，非淨非穢。不在
方，不離方；非有為，非無為。無示無說。不施不
慳，不戒不犯，不忍不恚，不進不怠，不定不亂，
不智不愚，不誠不欺，不來不去，不出不入，一切
言語道斷。非福田，非不福田；非應供養，非不應
供養；非取非捨。非有相，非無相。同真際，等法 12.125

性。不可稱，不可量，過諸稱量。非大非小，非見非聞，非覺非知，離眾結縛。等諸智，同眾生，於諸法無分別。一切無失，無濁無惱，無作無起，無生無滅。無畏無憂，無喜無厭無著。無已有，無當有，無今有。不可以一切言說分別顯示。世尊！如來身為若此，作如是觀。以斯觀者，名為正觀；若他觀者，名為邪觀。」

爾時，舍利弗問維摩詰：「汝於何沒而來生此？」

維摩詰言：「汝所得法有沒生乎？」

舍利弗言：「無沒生也。」

12.126 「若諸法無沒生相，云何問言：『汝於何沒而來生此？』於意云何？譬如幻師，幻作男女，寧沒生耶？」

舍利弗言：「無沒生也。汝豈不聞佛說諸法如幻相乎？」

答曰：「如是！若一切法如幻相者！云何問言：『汝於何沒而來生此？』舍利弗！沒者為虛誑法，敗壞之相；生者為虛誑法，相續之相。菩薩雖沒，不盡善本；雖生，不長諸惡。」

是時佛告舍利弗：「有國名妙喜，佛號無動。是維摩詰於彼國沒，而來生此。」

舍利弗言：「未曾有也。世尊！是人乃能捨清淨土，而來樂此多怒害處。」

12.127 維摩詰語舍利弗：「於意云何？日光出時與冥合乎？」

答曰：「不也！日光出時，即無眾冥。」

維摩詰言：「夫日何故行閻浮提？」

答曰：「欲以明照，為之除冥。」

維摩詰言：「菩薩如是！雖生不淨佛土，為化眾生故，不與愚闇而共合也，但滅眾生煩惱闇耳！」

是時大眾渴仰，欲見妙喜世界無動如來，及其菩薩、 12.128
聲聞之眾。佛知一切眾會所念，告維摩詰言：「善男子！為此眾會，現妙喜國無動如來，及諸菩薩、聲聞之眾，眾皆欲見。」

於是維摩詰心念：「吾當不起于座，接妙喜國，鐵圍山川溪谷江河，大海泉源，須彌諸山，及日月星宿、天龍鬼神梵天等宮，并諸菩薩、聲聞之眾，城邑聚落，男女大小，乃至無動如來，及菩提樹，諸妙蓮華，能於十方作佛事者；三道寶階從閻浮提，至忉利天，以此寶階，諸天來下，悉為禮敬無動如來，聽受經法。閻浮提人，亦登其階，上昇忉利，見彼諸天。妙喜世界成就如是無量功德，上至阿迦膩吒天，下至水際；以右手斷取，如陶家輪，入此世界，猶持華鬘，示一切眾。」作是念已，入於三昧，現神通力，以其右手斷取妙喜世界，置於此土。

彼得神通菩薩及聲聞眾，并餘天、人，俱發聲言： 12.129
「唯然世尊！誰取我去！願見救護。」

無動佛言：「非我所為，是維摩詰神力所作。」其餘未得神通者，不覺不知己之所往。妙喜世界，雖入此土，而不增減，於是世界亦不迫隘，如本無異。

爾時，釋迦牟尼佛告諸大眾：「汝等且觀妙喜世界無動如來，其國嚴飾，菩薩行淨，弟子清白。」

皆曰：「唯然已見。」

佛言：「若菩薩欲得如是清淨佛土，當學無動如來所行之道。」

現此妙喜國時，娑婆世界十四那由他人，發阿耨多羅三藐三菩提心，皆願生於妙喜佛土。釋迦牟尼佛即記之曰：「當生彼國。」時妙喜世界於此國土所應饒益，其事訖已，還復本處，舉眾皆見。

12.130 佛告舍利弗：「汝見此妙喜世界及無動佛不？」

「唯然已見，世尊！願使一切眾生得清淨土，如無動佛；獲神通力，如維摩詰。世尊！我等快得善利，得見是人親近供養。其諸眾生，若今現在，若佛滅後，聞此經者，亦得善利；況復聞已信解，受持讀誦解說，如法修行。若有手得是經典者，便為已得法寶之藏；若有讀誦解釋其義，如說修行，即為諸佛之所護念；其有供養如是人者，當知即為供養於佛；其有書持此經卷者，當知其室即有如來；若聞是經能隨喜者，斯人即為取一切智；若能信解此經，乃至一四句偈，為他說者，當知此人，即是受阿耨多羅三藐三菩提記。」

法供養品第十三

爾時，釋提桓因於大眾中白佛言：「世尊！我雖從佛及文殊師利聞百千經，未曾聞此不可思議，自在神通，決定實相經典。如我解佛所說義趣，若有眾生聞是經法，信解受持讀誦之者，必得是法不疑，何況如說修行？斯人即為閉眾惡趣，開諸善門，常為諸佛之所護念；降伏外學，摧滅魔怨；修治菩提，
安處道場；履踐如來所行之跡。世尊！若有受持讀 13.131
誦如說修行者，我當與諸眷屬供養給事；所在聚落城邑、山林曠野，有是經處，我亦與諸眷屬，聽受法故共到其所；其未信者，當令生信；其已信者，當為作護。」

佛言：「善哉，善哉！天帝！如汝所說，吾助爾喜。此經廣說過去、未來、現在諸佛不可思議阿耨多羅三藐三菩提。是故，天帝！若善男子、善女人，受持、讀誦、供養是經者，即為供養去、來、今佛。

「天帝！正使三千大千世界如來滿中，譬如甘蔗、 13.132
竹葦、稻麻、叢林；若有善男子、善女人，或一劫、

或減一劫，恭敬尊重，讚歎供養，奉諸所安，至諸佛滅後，以一一全身舍利起七寶塔，縱廣一四天下，高至梵天，表刹莊嚴；以一切華香、瓔珞、幢幡、伎樂微妙第一，若一劫、若減一劫，而供養之。於天帝意云何，其人植福，寧為多不？」

釋提桓因言：「多矣，世尊！彼之福德，若以百千億劫，說不能盡。」

佛告天帝：「當知是善男子、善女人，聞是不可思議解脫經典，信解受持，讀誦修行，福多於彼。所以者何？諸佛菩提皆從是生；菩提之相不可限量，以是因緣福不可量。」

13.133 佛告天帝：「過去無量阿僧祇劫，時世有佛，號曰藥王如來、應供、正遍知、明行足、善逝、世間解、無上士、調御丈夫、天人師、佛、世尊。世界名大莊嚴，劫曰莊嚴，佛壽二十小劫；其聲聞僧三十六億那由他；菩薩僧有十二億。

「天帝！是時有轉輪聖王，名曰寶蓋，七寶具足，主四天下。王有千子，端正勇健，能伏怨敵。爾時，寶蓋與其眷屬供養藥王如來，施諸所安，至滿五劫。過五劫已，告其千子：『汝等亦當如我，以深心供養於佛。』

13.134 「於是千子受父王命，供養藥王如來，復滿五劫，一切施安。其王一子，名曰月蓋，獨坐思惟：『寧有供養殊過此者？』以佛神力，空中有天曰：『善男子！法之供養勝諸供養。』即問：『何謂法之供養？』天曰：『汝可往問藥王如來，當廣為汝說法之供養。』

「即時月蓋王子行詣藥王如來，稽首佛足，却住一面，白佛言：『世尊！諸供養中，法供養勝。云何為法供養？』佛言：『善男子！法供養者，諸佛所 13.135
說深經，一切世間難信難受，微妙難見，清淨無染，非但分別思惟之所能得。菩薩法藏所攝，陀羅尼印印之。至不退轉，成就六度，善分別義，順菩提法，眾經之上。入大慈悲，離眾魔事，及諸邪見。順因緣法，無我，無人，無眾生，無壽命，空、無相、無作、無起。能令眾生坐於道場，而轉法輪，諸天、龍神、乾闥婆等，所共歎譽。能令眾生入佛法藏，攝諸賢聖一切智慧。說眾菩薩所行之道，依於諸法實相之義。明宣無常、苦、空、無我、寂滅之法，能救一切毀禁眾生；諸魔外道及貪著者，能使怖畏；諸佛賢聖所共稱歎。背生死苦，示涅槃樂，十方三世諸佛所說。若聞如是等經，信解受持讀誦，以方便力，為諸眾生分別解說，顯示分明，守護法故，是名法之供養。又於諸法如說修行，隨順十二 13.136
因緣，離諸邪見，得無生忍；決定無我無有眾生，而於因緣果報無違無諍，離諸我所。依於義，不依語；依於智，不依識；依了義經，不依不了義經；依於法，不依人。隨順法相，無所入，無所歸。無明畢竟滅故，諸行亦畢竟滅；乃至生畢竟滅故，老死亦畢竟滅。作如是觀，十二因緣，無有盡相，不復起見，是名最上法之供養。』」

佛告天帝：「王子月蓋從藥王佛聞如是法，得柔順 13.137
忍。即解寶衣嚴身之具，以供養佛，白佛言：『世尊！如來滅後，我當行法供養，守護正法。願以威神加哀建立，令我得降魔怨，修菩薩行。』佛知其深心所念，而記之曰：『汝於末後，守護法城。』

天帝！時王子月蓋，見法清淨，聞佛授記，以信出家，修集善法；精進不久，得五神通，逮菩薩道，
13.138 得陀羅尼，無斷辯才。於佛滅後，以其所得神通、總持、辯才之力，滿十小劫，藥王如來所轉法輪隨而分布。月蓋比丘以守護法，勤行精進，即於此身，化百萬億人於阿耨多羅三藐三菩提，立不退轉；十四那由他人，深發聲聞、辟支佛心；無量眾生得生天上。天帝！時王寶蓋豈異人乎？今現得佛，號寶炎如來；其王千子，即賢劫中千佛是也。從迦羅鳩孫馱為始得佛，最後如來號曰樓至。月蓋比丘，即我身是。如是，天帝！當知此要，以法供養於諸供養為上為最，第一無比。是故天帝！當以法之供養，供養於佛。」

囑累品第十四

於是佛告彌勒菩薩言：「彌勒！我今以是無量億阿僧祇劫所集阿耨多羅三藐三菩提法，付囑於汝。如是輩經，於佛滅後末世之中，汝等當以神力，廣宣流布於閻浮提，無令斷絕。所以者何？未來世中，當有善男子、善女人，及天、龍、鬼神、乾闥婆、羅剎等，發阿耨多羅三藐三菩提心，樂于大法；若使不聞如是等經，則失善利。如此輩人，聞是等經，必多信樂，發希有心，當以頂受，隨諸眾生所應得利，而為廣說。

「彌勒當知！菩薩有二相。何謂為二？一者，好於雜句文飾之事；二者，不畏深義如實能入。若好雜句文飾事者，當知是為新學菩薩；若於如是無染無著甚深經典，無有恐畏，能入其中，聞已心淨，受持讀誦，如說修行，當知是為久修道行。 14.139

「彌勒！復有二法，名新學者，不能決定於甚深法。何等為二？一者，所未聞深經，聞之驚怖生疑，不能隨順，毀謗不信，而作是言：『我初不聞。從何所來？』二者，若有護持解說如是深經者，不肯親近、供養、恭敬，或時於中說其過惡。有此二法，當知是為新學菩薩，為自毀傷，不能於深法中，調伏其心。

14.140 「彌勒！復有二法，菩薩雖信解深法，猶自毀傷，而不能得無生法忍。何等為二？一者，輕慢新學菩薩，而不教誨；二者，雖解深法，而取相分別。是為二法。」

彌勒菩薩聞說是已，白佛言：「世尊！未曾有也。如佛所說，我當遠離如斯之惡，奉持如來無數阿僧祇劫所集阿耨多羅三藐三菩提法。若未來世善男子、善女人求大乘者，當令手得如是等經，與其念力，使受持讀誦、為他廣說。世尊！若後末世，有能受持讀誦、為他說者，當知皆是彌勒神力之所建立。」

14.141 佛言：「善哉，善哉！彌勒！如汝所說，佛助爾喜。」

於是一切菩薩合掌白佛：「我等亦於如來滅後，十方國土廣宣流布阿耨多羅三藐三菩提法，復當開導諸說法者，令得是經。」

爾時，四天王白佛言：「世尊！在在處處、城邑聚落、山林曠野，有是經卷，讀誦解說者，我當率諸官屬，為聽法故，往詣其所，擁護其人，面百由旬，令無伺求得其便者。」

是時佛告阿難：「受持是經，廣宣流布。」

阿難言：「唯然！我已受持要者。世尊！當何名斯經？」

佛言：「阿難！是經名為『維摩詰所說』，亦名『不可思議解脫法門』，如是受持。」

佛說是經已，長者維摩詰、文殊師利、舍利弗、阿難等，及諸天、人、阿修羅一切大眾，聞佛所說，皆大歡喜。

INDEX

Notes on usage: A forward slash (/) or parentheses is used to indicate alternative terms or translations for the same concept.

Verse for Dedicating Merit

May the merit and virtue accrued
from this work
Adorn the Buddhas' Pure Lands,
Repaying the four kinds of benefactors
And aiding those suffering in the three paths.
May all who see and hear of this
Aspire to awaken to the Truth,
And when this life is over,
Be born together in the Land of Ultimate Bliss.

NAMO DHARMA PROTECTOR
WEITUO BODHISATTVA

DHARMA REALM BUDDHIST ASSOCIATION BRANCHES

USA

THE CITY OF TEN THOUSAND BUDDHAS
4951 Bodhi Way
Ukiah, CA 95482
TEL: (707) 462-0939
FAX: (707) 462-0949
www.drba.org

INSTITUTE FOR WORLD RELIGIONS (BERKELEY BUDDHIST MONASTERY)
2304 McKinley Avenue,
Berkeley, CA 94703
TEL: (510) 848-3440
www.berkeleymonastery.org

THE INTERNATIONAL TRANSLATION INSTITUTE
1777 Murchison Drive
Burlingame, CA 94010-4504
TEL: (650) 692-5912

BLESSINGS, PROSPERITY, & LONGEVITY MONASTERY
4140 Long Beach Boulevard
Long Beach, CA 90807
TEL: (562) 595-4966
www.bplmonastery.org

LONG BEACH SAGELY MONASTERY
3361 East Ocean Boulevard,
Long Beach, CA 90803
TEL/FAX: (562) 438-8902
www.longbeachmonastery.org

GOLD WHEEL MONASTERY
235 North Avenue 58,
Los Angeles, CA 90042
TEL: (323) 258-6668
www.goldwheel.org

THE CITY OF THE DHARMA REALM
1029 West Capitol Avenue
West Sacramento, CA 95691
TEL: (916) 374-8268
FAX: (916) 374-8234
www.cityofdharmarealm.org

GOLD MOUNTAIN MONASTERY
800 Sacramento Street
San Francisco, CA 94108
TEL: (415) 421-6117
FAX: (415) 788-6001
www.goldmountainmonastery.org

GOLD SAGE MONASTERY
11455 Clayton Road
San Jose, CA 95127
TEL: (408) 923-7243
FAX: (408) 923-1064
www.drbagsm.org/en

AVATAMSAKA VIHARA
9601 Seven Locks Road
Bethesda, MD 20817-9997
TEL/FAX: (301) 469-8300
www.avatamsakavihara.org

SNOW MOUNTAIN MONASTERY
P.O. Box 272
50924 Index-Galena Road
Index, WA 98256
TEL: (360) 799-0699
FAX: (815) 346-9141
smm.drba.org

GOLD SUMMIT MONASTERY
233 1st Avenue West
Seattle, WA 98119
TEL: (206) 284-6690
www.goldsummitmonastery.org

CANADA

AVATAMSAKA MONASTERY
1009 4th Avenue S.W.
Calgary, AB T2P OK 8 Canada
TEL: (403) 234-0644
www.avatamsaka.ca

GOLD BUDDHA MONASTERY
248 East 11th Avenue,
Vancouver, B.C. V5T 2C3 Canada
TEL: (604) 709-0248
FAX: (604) 684-3754
www.gbm-online.com

AUSTRALIA

GOLD COAST DHARMA REALM
106 Bonogin Road
Mudgeeraba, Queensland 4213
Australia
TEL: +61 (7) 5522-8788
FAX: +61 (7) 5522-7822
www.gcdr.org.au

HONG KONG

BUDDHIST LECTURE HALL
31 Wong Nei Chong Road,
Top Floor
Happy Valley, Hong Kong, China
TEL: +852 2572-7644
FAX: +852 2572-2850

CIXING CHAN MONASTERY
Lantou Island, Man Cheung Po
Hong Kong, China
TEL: +852 2985-5159

MALAYSIA

DHARMA REALM GUAN YIN
SAGELY MONASTERY
(KUN YAM THONG TEMPLE)
PRAJNA GUANYIN
SAGELY MONASTERY
161, Jalan Ampang
50450 Kuala Lumpur
West Malaysia
TEL: +60 (3) 2164-8055
FAX: +60 (3) 2163-7118

FA YUAN MONASTERY
1, Jalan Utama
Taman Serdang Raya
43300 Seri Kembangan

Selangor Darul Ehsan,
West Malaysia
TEL: +60 (3) 8958-5668

PERAK BRANCH
25-33, Jalan Kampar Permai 1
Taman Kampar Permai
31900 Kampar, Perak
West Malaysia
Tel: +6019 785 9138

PENANG BRANCH
32-32C, Jalan Tan Sri
Teh Ewe Lim
11600 Jelutong Penang
Malaysia
TEL: +60 (4) 281-7728
FAX: +60 (4) 281-7798

GUAN YIN SAGELY MONASTERY
166A Jalan Temiang
70200 Seremban Negeri Sembilan
West Malaysia
TEL/FAX: +60 (6) 761-1988

LOTUS VIHARA
136 Jalan Sekolah
45600 Batang Berjuntai, Selangor
Darul Ehsan, West Malaysia
TEL: (03) 3271-9439

TAIWAN

DHARMA REALM BUDDHIST BOOKS DISTRIBUTION SOCIETY
11th Floor
85 Zhongxiao E. Road, Sec. 6
Taipei 11575, Taiwan R.O.C.
TEL: +866 (2) 2786-3022
FAX: +866 (2) 2786-2674

DHARMA REALM SAGELY MONASTERY
No. 20, Dongxi Shanzhuang,
Liugui Dist.
Gaoxiong 844, Taiwan, R.O.C.
TEL: +866 (7) 689-3713
FAX: +866 (7) 689-3870

AMITABHA MONASTERY
No. 126, Fuji Street,
Chinan Village, Shoufeng
Hualian County 974, Taiwan, R.O.C.
TEL: +866 (3) 865-1956
FAX: +866 (3) 865-3426

SUBSIDIARY ORGANIZATIONS

BUDDHIST TEXT TRANSLATION SOCIETY
City of Ten Thousand Buddhas
4951 Bodhi Way
Ukiah, CA 95482 USA
WEB: www.buddhisttexts.org
EMAIL: info@buddhisttexts.org
CATALOG: www.bttsonline.org

DHARMA REALM BUDDHIST UNIVERSITY
City of Ten Thousand Buddhas
4951 Bodhi Way
Ukiah, CA 95482 USA
www.drbu.org

DHARMA REALM OUTREACH
City of Ten Thousand Buddhas
outreach@drba.org